# FREEMASONRY
## CHARACTER, CLAIMS & PRACTICAL WORKINGS OF

by

# REV. C. G. FINNEY
Late President of Orbelin College, Ohio

Buffalo, New York
14208
eeworldinc@yahoo.com

*FREEMASONRY : CHARACTER, CLAIMS & PRACTICAL WORKINGS OF.* Copyright © by C.G. Finney. All rights reserved. No part of this book may be reproduced in any form or by any means including electronic, mechanical or photocopying or stored in a retrieval system without permission in writing from the publisher.

ISBN: 978-1-61759-027-6

COVER DESIGN: *Yahaira Zapata*

About the Front Cover: The All-seeing eye and the skull. The skull originally made an appearance in eighteenth century French Freemasonry, symbolic of death and resurrection.

About the Back Cover: The Masonic ceremonial sword. An instrument of justice, truth and equality.

Formally published by
A&B Publishers Group
Brooklyn, New York
ISBN 1-881316-89-0

Reprinted 2011 by

**EWORLD INC.**

**Buffalo, New York
14208
eeworldinc@yahoo.com**

11 12 13 14    5 4 3 2 1
Manufactured and Printed in the United States

# PREFACE.

In few words I wish to state what are *not* and **what are** my reasons for writing this book.
1. It is *not* that I have any quarrel or controversy with any member of the Masonic Order. No one of them can justly accuse me of any personal ill-will or unkindness.
2. It is *not* because I am fond of controversy—I am not. Although I have been compelled to engage in much discussion, still I have always dreaded and endeavored to avoid the *spirit* and even the *form* of controversy.
3. It is *not* because I disregard the sensibilty of Freemasons upon the question of their pet institution, and am quite willing to arouse their enmity by exposing it. I value the good opinion and good wishes of Freemasons as I do those of other men, and have no disposition to capriciously or wantonly assail what they regard with so much favor.
4. It is *not* because I am willing, if I can dutifully avoid it, to render any member of the Fraternity odious. But my reasons are:
1. I wish, if *possible*, to arrest the spread of this great evil, by giving the public, at least, so much information upon this subject as to induce them to examine and understand the true character and tendency of the institution.
2. I wish, if possible, to arouse the *young men* who are Freemasons, to consider the inevitable consequences of such a horrible trifling with the most solemn oaths, as is constantly practiced by Freemasons. Such a course must, and does, as a matter of fact, grieve the Holy Spirit, sear the conscience, and harden the heart.
3. I wish to induce the young men who are not Freemasons "*to look before they leap,*" and not be deceived and committed, as thousands have been, before they were at all aware of the true nature of the institution of Freemasonry

## PREFACE.

4. I, with the many, have been remiss in suffering a new generation to grow up in ignorance of the character of Freemasonry, as it was fully revealed to us who are now old. We have greatly erred in not preserving and handing down to the rising generation the *literature* upon this subject, with which we were made familiar forty years ago. For *one*, I must not continue this remissness.

5. Because I know that nothing but correct information is wanting to banish this institution from wholesome society. This has been abundantly proven. As soon as Freemasons saw that their secrets were made public, they abandoned their lodges for very shame. With such oaths upon their souls, they could not face the frown of an indignant public, already aware of their true position.

6. Freemasons exhort each other to maintain a dignified silence and are exhorted not to enter into controversy with opposers of Freemasonry. The reasons are obvious to those who are informed. We know why they are silent if they are so, and why they will not enter the field of controversy and attempt to justify their institution. Let anyone examine the question and he will see why they make no attempt to justify Freemasonry as it is revealed in the books from which I have quoted. I greatly desire to have the public, and especially the church of Christ, understand what Freemasonry is. Then let them act as duty requires.

7. Should I be asked why I have not spoken out upon this subject before, I reply that until the question was sprung upon us in this place a year ago, I was not at all aware that Freemasonry had been disinterred and was alive, and stalking abroad over the face of the whole land.

8. This book contains the numbers published in in the Independent last year,. These are revised, enlarged and rearranged. To these are added eight numbers not heretofore published.

9. I have said in the body of the work, and say also in this preface, that I have no pecuniary intent in the sale of this work. I have not written for money, nor for fame. I shall get neither for my pains. I desire only to do good.  C. G. FINNEY.

# CONTENTS.

### CHAPTER I.
Introduction, . . . . . . . . . . . . 5

### CHAPTER II.
Scrap of History, . . . . . . . . . . . . 9

### CHAPTER III.
How known, . . . . . . . . . . . . 23

### CHAPTER IV.
Credibility of the Books revealing Masonry, . . . 30

### CHAPTER V.
Examination of the Books revealing Masonry, . . . 63

### CHAPTER VI.
Master's Degree, . . . . . . . . . . . . 70

### CHAPTER VII.
Royal Arch Degree, . . . . . . . . . . . . 89

## CONTENTS.

### CHAPTER VIII.
Sworn to Persecute, . . . . . . . . 102

### CHAPTER IX.
Awful Profanity of Masonic Oaths, . . . . 108

### CHAPTER X.
Perverse and Profane Use of the Holy Bible, . . . 123

### CHAPTER XI.
Freemasonry imposes on the Ignorant, . . . . . 138

### CHAPTER XII.
Masonry susceptible of Change only by Additions, . 152

### CHAPTER XIII.
The Claim of Freemasonry to Antiquity is False, . . 170

### CHAPTER XIV.
The boasted Benevolence of Masons a Sham, . . . 184

### CHAPTER XV.
Freemasonry is a False Religion, . . . . . . . 199

### CHAPTER XVI.
The Argument that Great and Good Men have been and are Freemasons examined, 220

CONTENTS.

## CHAPTER XVII.
Masonic Oaths are Unlawful and Void, . . . . . 229

## CHAPTER XVIII.
Why Freemasons resort to Threats and refuse to discuss their Principles, . . . . . . . . . . . 239

## CHAPTER XIX.
Relations of Masonry to the Church of Christ, . . . 255

## CHAPTER XX.
Conclusion, . . . . . . . . . . . . . . . 268

## Charles G. Finney

PRES. Charles G. Finney died in 1875, at the age of eighty-three years.

He began his public life as a lawyer and a freemason; he closed it as one of the greatest evangelists this country and Europe had ever known; as an author and theological teacher of renown; as president of a great college, which had grown up under his administration. He was widely known as an abolishionist and as a seceding Mason.

The practical results of his life-work increasingly commend themselves, and give testimony to that work as a remarkable uplifting and spiritualizing force. His best-known published writings are: Lectures on Revivals of Religion; Lectures to Professing Christians; Lectures on Theology; Character, Claims and Practical Workings of Freemasonry; Memoirs — An Autobiography.

## CHAPTER I.

### INTRODUCTORY

IT is high time that the Church of Christ was awake to the character and tendency of Freemasonry.

Forty years ago we supposed that it was dead, and had no idea that it could ever revive. But, strange to tell, while we were busy in getting rid of slavery, Freemasonry has revived, and extended its bounds most alarmingly. I propose to write a series of articles, giving my views of the character and tendency of the institution.

I know something about it, for I have been a Freemason myself. Soon after I was twenty-one years of age, and while in Connecticut at school, an old uncle of mine persuaded me to join the Freemasons, representing that, as I was from home and much among strangers, it would be of service to me, because if a Freemason I should find friends everywhere. The lodge in that place was but a Master's lodge.

I therefore took three degrees, or as far as what they call "the sublime degree of Master Mason." When I returned to the State of New York, to enter upon the study of law, I found at Adams, where I resided, a Masonic lodge and united with them. I soon became secretary of the lodge, and met regularly with the lodge. When I took especially the Master's degree I was struck with one part of the obligation, or oath, as not being sound either in a political or moral point of view.

However, I had been brought up with very few religious privileges, and had but slight knowledge on moral subjects; and I was not, therefore, greatly shocked, at the time, with the immorality of anything through which I passed. The lodge where I took my degrees was composed, I believe, mostly of professed Christians. But when I came to join the lodge at Adams I found that the Master of the lodge was a deist. At this distance of time I can not be certain whether the deist to whom I refer, Eliphalet Edmunds, was Master of the lodge when I first joined. My best recollection is that Captain Goodell was Master when I first joined the lodge at Adams, and that Judge Edmunds was Master at the time of my conversion to Christ. I am certain that deism was no objection to any man becoming a member or a Master of the lodge. There were in that lodge some as thoroughly irreligious men as I have ever associated with anywhere, and men with whom I never would have associated had they not been Freemasons. I do not recollect that any Christian men belonged to that lodge at the time I joined it. There were some very profane men who belonged to it, and some men of very intemperate habits.

As I paid the strictest attention to what they called their lectures and teachings, I became what they call "a *bright* Mason;" that is, as far as I went, I committed to memory their *oral* teachings—for they had no other.

The oaths, or obligations, were familiar to me, as was everything else that belonged to those three degrees that I had taken.

I had belonged to the lodge in Adams nearly four years when I was converted to Christ. During the struggle of conviction of sin through which I passed, I do not recollect that the question of Freemasonry ever occurred to my mind. The season that I called properly my conviction of sin was short. My exercises were pungent, and I very soon obtained hope in Christ.

Soon after my conversion the evening came

for attendance upon the lodge. I went. They of course, were aware that I had become a Christian, and the Master of the lodge called upon me to open the lodge with prayer. I did so, and poured out my heart to the Lord for blessings upon the lodge. I observed that it created a considerable excitement. The evening passed away, and at the close of the lodge I was requested to pray again. I did so, and retired, but much depressed in spirit. I soon found that I was completely converted *from* Freemasonry *to* Christ, and that I could have no fellowship with any of the proceedings of the lodge. Its oaths appeared to me to be monstrously profane and barbarous.

At that time I did not know how much I had been imposed upon by many of the pretensions of Masonry. But upon reflection and examination, and after a severe struggle and earnest prayer, I found that I could not consistently remain with them. My new life instinctively and irresistibly recoiled from any fellowship with what I then regarded as "the unfruitful works of darkness."

Without consulting any person, I finally went to the lodge and requested my discharge. After manifesting considerable reluctance, they granted my request. My mind was made up. Withdraw from them I must, with their consent if I might, without their consent if I must. Of this I said nothing; but some way it came to be known that I had withdrawn from them. This created some little feeling among them. They, therefore, planned a Masonic celebration or festival. I do not recollect exactly what it was. But they sent a committee to me, requesting me to deliver an oration on the occasion. I quietly declined to do so; informing the committee that I could not conscientiously in anywise do what would manifest my approval of the institution, or sympathy with it. However, at that time, and for years afterward, I remained silent and said nothing against the institution; for I had not then so well considered the matter as to regard my Masonic oaths as utterly null and void. But from that time I never allowed myself to be recognized as a Freemason anywhere. This was a few years before the revelations of Freemasonry, by William Morgan, were published. When that book was published, I was asked if it was a true revelation of Freemasonry. I replied that it was, so far as I knew anything about it; and that, as nearly as I could recollect, it was a *verbatim* revelation of the first three degrees as I had myself taken them. I replied in this way because I saw, of course, that as the thing was published, and no longer a secret, I could not be under any obligations to keep it a secret, unless I could be under an obligation to lie, and to lie *perpetually*, by denying that that which had been published was truly Freemasonry.

I knew that I could be under no obligations to be guilty of a perpetual falsehood, and that I really made no revelation of any secret when I frankly acknowledged that that which had been published was a true account of the institution, and a true *expose* of their oaths, principles and proceedings.

Afterward I considered it more thoroughly, and was most perfectly convinced that I had no right to adhere to the institution, or to appear to do so; and that I was bound, whenever the occasion arose, to speak my mind freely in regard to it, and to renounce the horrid oaths I had taken.

On reflection and examination, I found that I had been grossly deceived and imposed upon. I had been led to suppose that there were some very important secrets to be communicated to me. But in this respect I found myself entirely disappointed.

Indeed, I came to the deliberate conclusion, and could not avoid doing so, that my oaths had been procured by fraud and misrepresentations, and that the institution was in no respect what I had been previously informed it was.

And, as I have had the means of examining it more thoroughly, it has become more and more irresistibly plain to my convictions that the institution is highly dangerous to the State, and in every way injurious to the Church of Christ.

This I expect to show in detail should I be spared to finish the articles which I contemplate writing. But in my next it will be in place to inquire, *How are the public to know what Freemasonry really is?*

After this inquiry is settled, we shall be prepared to enter upon an examination of its *claims*, its *principles*, and its *tendency*.

## CHAPTER II.

### SCRAP OF HISTORY.

IN this number I must remind readers of some facts that occurred about forty years ago; which, as matters of history, though then well-known to thousands, are probably now unknown to the great majority of our citizens. Elderly men and women, especially in the Northern States, will almost universally remember the murder of William Morgan by Freemasons, and many facts connected with that terrible tragedy. But, as much pains have been taken by Freemasons to rid the world of the books and pamphlets, and every vestige of writing relating to that subject, by far the larger number of young people seem to be entirely ignorant that such facts ever occurred. I will state them as briefly as possible.

About forty year ago, an estimable man by the name of William Morgan, then residing in Batavia, N. Y., being a Freemason, after much reflection, made up his mind that it was his duty to publish Freemasonry to the world. He regarded it as highly injurious to the cause of Christ, and as eminently dangerous to the government of our country, and I suppose was aware, as Masons generally were at that time, that nearly all the civil offices in the country were in the hands of Freemasons; and that the press was completely under their control, and almost altogether in their hands. Masons at that time *boasted* that all the civil offices in the country were in their hands. I believe that all the civil offices in the county where I resided while I belonged to them, were in their hands I do not recollect a magistrate, or a constable, or sheriff in that county that was not at that time a Freemason.

A publisher by the name of Miller, also residing in Batavia, agreed to publish what Mr. Morgan would write. This, coming to be known to Freemasons, led them to conspire for his destruction. This, as we shall see, was only in accordance with their oaths. By their oaths they were *bound* to seek his destruction, and to execute upon him the penalty of those oaths.

They kidnapped Morgan and for a time concealed him in the magazine of the United States Fort—Fort Niagara, at the mouth of Niagara River, where it empties into Lake

Ontario. They kept him there until they could arrange to dispatch him. In the meantime, the greatest efforts were made to discover his whereabouts, and what the Masons had done with him. Strong suspicions came finally to be entertained that he was confined in that fort; and the Masons, finding that those suspicions were abroad, hastened his death. Two or three have since, upon their death-bed, confessed their part in the transaction. They drowned him in the Niagara River. The account of the manner in which this was done will be found in a book published by Elder Stearns, a Baptist elder. The book is entitled "Stearns on Masonry." It contains the death-bed confession of one of the murderers of William Morgan. On page 311, of that work, you will find that confession. But as many of my readers have not access to that work, I take the liberty to quote it entire, as follows:

"CONFESSION.

"THE MURDER OF WILLIAM MORGAN, CONFESSED BY THE MAN WHO, WITH HIS OWN HANDS, PUSHED HIM OUT OF THE BOAT INTO NIAGARA RIVER!

"The following account of that tragical scene is taken from a pamphlet entitled, 'Confession of the murder of William Morgan, as taken down by Dr. John L. Emery, of Racine County Wisconsin, in the summer of 1848, and now (1849) first given to the public:'

"This 'Confession' was taken down as related by Henry L. Valance, who acknowledges himself to have been one of the three who were selected to make a final disposition of the ill-fated victim of masonic vengeance. This confession it seems was made to his physicians, and in view of his approaching dissolution, and published after his decease.

"After committing that horrid deed he was as might well be expected, an unhappy man by day and by night. He was much like Cain — 'a fugitive and a vagabond.' To use his own words, 'Go where I would, or do what I would, it was impossible for me to throw off the consciousness of crime. If the mark of Cain was not upon me, the curse of the first murderer was — the blood-stain was upon my hands and could not be washed out.'

"He therefore commences his confession thus: — 'My last hour is approaching; and as the things of this world fade from my mental sight, I feel the necessity of making, as far as in my power lies, that atonement which every violator of the great law of right owes to his fellow men.' In this violation of law, he says, 'I allude to the abduction and murder of the ill-fated William Morgan.'

"He proceeds with an interesting narrative of the proceedings of the fraternity in reference to Morgan, while he was incarcerated in the magazine of Fort Niagara. I have room for a few extracts only, showing the final disposition of their alleged criminal. Many consultations were held, 'many plans proposed and discussed, and rejected.' At length being driven to the necessity of doing something immediately for fear of being exposed, it was resolved in a council of eight, that he must die: must be consigned to a 'confinement from which there is no possibility of escape — THE GRAVE.' Three of their number were to be selected by ballot to execute the deed. 'Eight pieces of paper were procured, five of which were to remain blank, while the letter D was written on the others. These pieces of paper were placed in a large box, from which each man was to draw one at the same moment. After drawing we were all to separate, without looking at the paper that each held in his hand. So soon as we had arrived at certain distances from the place of rendezvous, the tickets were to be examined, and those who held blanks were to return instantly to their homes; and those who should hold marked tickets were to proceed to the fort at midnight, and there put Morgan to death, in such a manner as should seem to themselves most fitting.' Mr. Valance was one of the three who drew the ballots on which was the signal letter. He returned to the fort, where he was joined by his two companions, who had drawn the death tickets. Arrangements were made immediately for executing the sentence passed upon their prisoner, which was to sink him in the river with weights; in hope, says Mr. Valance, 'that he and our crime alike would thus be buried beneath the waves.' His part was to proceed to the magazine where Morgan was confined, and announce to him his fate—theirs was to procure a boat and weights with which to sink him. Morgan, on being informed of their proceedings against him, demanded by what authority they had condemned him, and who were his judges. 'He commenced wringing his hands, and talking of his wife and children, the recollections of whom, in that awful hour, terribly affected him. His wife, he said, was young and inexperienced, and his children were but infants; what would become of them were he cut off, and they even ignorant of his fate?' What husband and father would not be 'terribly affected' under such circumstances—to be cut off from among the living in this inhuman manner?

"Mr. V.'s comrades returned, and informed him that they had procured the boat and weights, and that all things were in readiness on their part. Morgan was told that all his remonstrances were idle, that die he must, and that soon, even before the morning light. The feelings of the husband and father were still strong within him, and he continued to plead on behalf of his family. They gave him one half hour to prepare for his 'inevitable fate.' They retired from the magazine and left him. 'How Morgan passed that time,' says Mr. Valance, 'I cannot tell, but everything was quiet as the tomb within.' At the expiration of the allotted time, they entered the magazine, laid hold of their victim, 'bound his hands behind him, and placed a gag in his mouth.' They then led him forth to execution. 'A short time,' says this murderer, 'brought us to the boat, and we all entered it—Morgan being placed in the bow with myself, along side of him. My comrades took the oars, and the boat was rapidly forced out into the river. The night was pitch dark, we could scarcely see a yard before us, and therefore was the time admirably adapted to our hellish purpose.' Having reached a proper distance from the shore, the oarsmen ceased their labors. The weights were all secured together by a strong cord, and another cord of equal strength, and of several yards in length, proceeded from that. 'This cord,' says Mr. V., 'I took in my hand [did not that hand tremble?] and fastened it around the body of Morgan, just above his hips, using all my skill to make it fast, so that it would hold. Then, in a whisper, I bade the unhappy man to stand up, and after a momentary hesitation he complied with my order. He stood close to the head of the boat, and there was just length enough of rope from his person to the weights to prevent any strain, while he was standing. I then requested one of my associates to assist me in lifting the weights from the bottom to the side of the boat, while the others steadied her from the stern. This was done, and, as Morgan was standing with his back toward me, I approached him, and gave him a strong push with both my hands, which were placed on the middle of his back. He fell forward, carrying the weights with him, and the waters closed over the mass. We remained quiet for two or three minutes, when my companions, without saying a word, resumed their places, and rowed the boat to the place from which they had taken it.'"

They also kidnapped Mr. Miller, the publisher; but the citizens of Batavia, finding it out, pursued the kidnappers, and finally rescued him.

The courts of justice found themselves entirely unable to make any headway against the wide-spread conspiracy that was formed among Masons in respect to this matter.

These are matters of record. It was found that they could do nothing with the courts, with the sheriffs, with the witnesses, or with the jurors; and all their efforts were for a time entirely impotent. Indeed, they never were able to *prove* the murder of Morgan, and bring it home to the individuals who perpetrated it.

But Mr. Morgan had published Freemasonry to the world. The greatest pains were taken by Masons to cover up the transaction, and as far as possible to deceive the public in regard to the fact that Mr. Morgan had published Masonry as it really is.

Masons themselves, as is affirmed by the very best authority, published two spurious editions of Morgan's book, and circulated them as the true edition which Morgan had published. These editions were designed to deceive Masons who had never seen Morgan's edition, and thus to enable them to say that it was not a true revelation of Masonry

In consequence of the publication of Morgan's book, and the revelations that were made in regard to the kidnapping and murdering of Mr. Morgan, great numbers of Masons were led to consider the subject more fully than they had done; and the conscientious among them almost universally renounced Masonry altogether. I believe that about two thousand lodges, as a consequence of these revelations, were suspended.

The ex-president of a Western college, who is himself a Freemason, has recently published some very important information on the subject, though he justifies Masonry. He says that, out of a little more than fifty thousand Masons in the United States at that time, forty-five thousand turned their backs upon the lodge to enter the lodge no more. Conventions were called of Masons that were disposed to renounce it. One was held at Leroy, another at Philadelphia, and others at other places, I do not now remember where. The men composing these conventions made public confession of their relation to the institution, and publicly renounced it. At one of these large conventions they appointed a committee to superintend the publication of Masonry in all its degrees. This committee was composed of men of first-rate character, and men quite generally known to the public. Elder Bernard, a Baptist elder in good standing, was one of this committee; and he, with the assistance of his brethren who had been appointed to this work, obtained an accurate version of some forty eight degrees. He published also the proceedings of those conventions, and much concerning the efforts that were made by the courts to search the matter to the bottom, and also several speeches that were made by prominent men in the State of New York. This work was entitled "Light on Masonry." In this work any person who is disposed may get a very correct view of what Freemasonry really is. This and sundry other reliable works on Freemasonry may be had at Godrich's, and Fitch & Fairchild's bookstores, in Oberlin. In saying this, it is proper to add that I have no direct or indirect pecuniary interest in the sale of those or of any book on Freemasonry whatever, nor shall I have in the sale of this which I am now preparing for the press. Freemasons shall not with truth accuse me of self-interest in exposing their institution.

Before the publication of "Bernard's Light on Masonry," great pains were taken to secure the most accurate knowledge of the degrees published by the committee, as the reader of that work will see, if he reads the book through

An account of all these matters will be found in "Light on Masonry," to which I have referred. In the Northern or non-slaveholding States Masonry was almost universally renounced at that time. But it was found that it had taken so deep a root that in all New England there was scarcely a newspaper in which the death of William Morgan, and the circumstances connected therewith, could be published. This was so generally true throughout all the North that newspapers had to be everywhere established for the purpose of making the disclosures that were necessary in regard to its true character and tendency. The same game is being played over again at the present day. The "Cynosure," the new anti masonic paper published at Chicago, is constantly intercepted on its way to subscribers. Four of its first six numbers failed to reach me, and now in December, 1868, I have received no number later than the sixth. The editor informs me that the numbers are constantly intercepted. The public will be forced to learn what a lawless and hideous institution Freemasonry is. But at present I refrain from saying more on this point.

It was found that Masonry so completely baffled the courts of law, and obstructed the course of justice, that it was forced into politics; and for a time the anti-masonic sentiment of the Northern States carried all before it. Almost all Masons became ashamed of it, felt themselves disgraced by having any connection with it, and publicly renounced it. If they did not publish any renunciation, they suspended their lodges, had no more to do with it, and did not pretend to deny that Masonry had been published.

Now these facts were so notorious, so universally known and confessed, that those of us who were acquainted with them at the time had no idea that Masonry would have the impudence ever again to claim any public respect. I should just as soon expect slavery to be re-established in this country, and become more popular than ever before—to take possession of the Government and of all the civil offices, and to grow bold, impudent, and defiant—as I should have expected that Masonry would achieve what it has. When the subject of Freemasonry was first forced upon our churches in Oberlin, for discussion and action, I can not ex press the astonishment, grief and indignation that I felt on hearing professed Christian Freemasons deny either expressly or by irresistible implication that Morgan and others had truly revealed the secrets of Freemasonry. But a few years ago such denial would have ruined the character of any intelligent man, not to say of a professed Christian.

But I must say, also, that Masonry itself has its literature. Many bombastic and spread-eagle books have been published in its favor. They never attempt to justify it as it is revealed in "Light on Masonry," nor reply by argument to the attacks that have been so successfully made upon it; neither have they pretended to reveal its secrets. But they have eulogized it in a manner that is utterly nauseating to those that understand what it really is. But these books have been circulated among the young, and have no doubt led thousands and scores of thousands of young men into the Masonic ranks, who, but for these miserable productions, would never have thought of taking such a step.

## CHAPTER III.

## HOW KNOWN.

WE are prepared in this number to take up the question, *How are the public to know what Freemasonry really is?* This we may answer.

1. *Negatively.* (1.) Masonry cannot be known from a perusal of the eulogistic books which adhering Masons have written. Of course they are under oath in no way whatever to reveal the secrets of Masonry. But it is their *secrets* that the public are concerned to know Now their eulogistic books, as any one may know who will examine them, are silly, and for the most part little better than twaddle. If we read their orations and sermons that have been published in support of Masonry, and the books that they have written, we shall find much that is silly, much that is false, and a great deal more that is mere bombast and rhodomontade. I do not say this rashly. Any person who will examine the subject for himself must admit that this language is strictly

true. But shall have occasion hereafter when we come to examine the character of the institution, to show more clearly the utter ignorance or dishonesty of the men who have eulogized it.

Let it be understood, then, that *adhering* Masons do not profess to publish their *secrets* And that which the country and the church are particularly interested to understand they never publish—their oaths, for example; and, therefore, we cannot tell from what they write what they are under oath to do.

(2.) *We cannot learn what Masonry is from the oral testimony of adhering Masons.*

Let it be pondered well that every one of them is under oath to conceal and in no way whatever to reveal the secrets of the order. This Freemasons do not deny. Hence, if they are asked if the books in which Masonry has been published are true, they will either evade the question or else they will lie; *and they are under oath to do so.*

Observe, *adhering* Masons are the men who still acknowledge the binding obligation of their oaths. Now, if they are asked if those books truly reveal Masonry, they consider themselves under an obligation to deny it, if they say anything about it. And, as they are well aware that to *refuse to say anything about* it is a *virtual acknowledgment* that the books are true, and would therefore be an *indirect* revelation of Masonry; they will almost universally deny that the books are true. Some of them are ashamed to say anything more than that there is some truth and a great deal of falsehood in them.

(3.) As they are under oath to conceal the secrets of Masonry, and in no wise whatever to reveal any part of them, their testimony in regard to the truthfulness or untruthfulness of those books is of no value whatever. It is mere madness to receive the testimony of men who are under oath, and under the most horrid oaths that can be taken—oaths sustained by the most terrific penalties that can be named to conceal their secrets and to deny that they have been published, and that those books contain them—I say it is downright madness to receive the testimony of such men, it matters not who they are. Masons have no right to expect an intelligent person to believe their denials that these books have truly revealed Masonry. Nor have they a right to complain if we reject their testimony. What would they have us do? Shall we believe the testimony of men who admit that they are under oath to conceal and never in any way reveal the secrets of their order, when they deny that their secrets are revealed in certain books, and shall we ignore the testimony of thousands who have conscientiously renounced those horrid oaths, at the hazard of their lives, and declared with one accord, and many of them under the sanction of judicial oaths lawfully administered, that Morgan, Bernard and others have truly revealed the secrets of Freemasonry? There are at this day thousands of most conscientious men who are ready to testify on oath that those books contain a substantially correct exposition of Freemasonry as it was and is. I say again that Freemasons have no right to expect us to believe their denials; for while they adhere to Masonry they are under oath to "conceal and never reveal" any part of its secrets and of course they must *expressly* or *impliedly* deny every revelation of its secrets that can be made. *Would they have us stultify ourselves by receiving their testimony?*

2. *Positively.* *How, then, are we to know what Masonry is?* I answer: (1.) From the published and oral testimony of those who have taken the degrees; and afterward, from conscientious motives, have confessed their error, and have publicly renounced Masonry. But it has been said that these are *perjured* men, and therefore not at all to be believed. But let it be remarked that this very accusa-

tion is an admission that they have published
the truth; for, unless they have published the
secrets of Masonry *truly*, they have violated
no Masonic oath. Therefore, when Masons accuse them of being perjured, the very objection
which they make to the testimony of these
witnesses is an acknowledgment on the part of
Masons themselves that they have truly published their secrets.

But again. If to reveal the secrets of Masonry be perjury, it follows that to accuse the
revealers of Masonry of perjury, is itself perjury; because by their accusation they tacitly
admit that that which has been published is
truly a revelation of Masonry, and therefore
their accusation is a violation of their oath of secrecy. Let it then be understood that the very
objection to these witnesses, that they have
committed perjury, is itself an acknowledgment
that the witnesses are entirely credible, and
have revealed Masonry as it is. And not only
so—but in bringing forward the objection,
they commit perjury themselves, if it be perjury
to reveal their secrets; because, as I have said,
in accusing the witnesses of perjury, they add
*their* testimony to the fact that these witnesses
have published Masonry as it is. So that
by their own testimony, in bringing this
charge of perjury, they themselves swell the

number of witnesses to the truthfulness of these revelations.

(2.) *Renouncing Masons are the best possible witnesses by whom to prove what Masonry really is.* (*a.*) They are *competent* witnesses. They testify from *their own personal knowledge of what it is.* (*b.*) They are in the highest degree *credible* witnesses. First, because they *testify against themselves.* They confess their own wrong in having taken those terrible oaths, and in having had any part in sustaining the institution. Secondly, their testimony is given with the certainty of incurring a most unrelenting persecution. *Adhering* Freemasons are under oath to persecute them, to destroy their characters, and to seek to bring them to condign punishment. *This we shall see when we come to examine the books.* *Adhering* Masons have persecuted, and still persecute, those that reveal their secrets, just as far as they dare. They are in the highest degree intolerant, and this every Mason knows. In a recent number of their great Masonic organ, published in New York, they advise the Masons in Oberlin in no way to patronize those who oppose them. Those who renounce Masonry are well aware of their danger. But, notwithstanding, they are constrained by their consciences, by the fear and love of God, and by regard to the interests of their country, to renounce and expose it. Now, surely, witnesses that testify under such circumstances are entitled to credit; especially as they could have had no conceivable motive for deceiving the public. Their testimony was *wrung* from them by conscience. And the authors of the books that I have named, together with several others—such as Richardson, Stearns, and Mr Allyn, and I know not how many others—are sustained by the testimony of *forty-five thousand* who publicly renounced Masonry, out of a little more than fifty thousand that composed the whole number of Freemasons then in the United States. Now, it should be well remembered that the five thousand who still adhered belonged almost altogether to the slaveholding States, and had peculiar reasons for still adhering to the institution of Masonry. And, further, let it be distinctly observed that, as they adhered to Masonry, their testimony is null, because they still regarded themselves as under oath in no wise to reveal their secrets; consequently, they would, of course, deny that these books had truly revealed Masonry. I say again, it is mere madness to receive their testimony.

## CHAPTER IV

## CREDIBILITY OF THE BOOKS REVEALING FREEMASONRY.

FURTHER observe: (3.) The credibility of these books in which Masonry is revealed is evident from the following considerations:

(*a.*) *The murder of Morgan by Freemasons was an emphatic acknowledgment that he had revealed their secrets.* For, if he had not, he had not incurred the penalty of Masonic obligations. They murdered him because he had truly revealed their secrets; and they could have had no motive whatever for murdering him if he had not done so.

(*b.*) The credibility of these books is further sustained by the fact that *adhering* Masons did then, and have *always*, justified the murder of Morgan as that which their oaths obliged them to do. They have said that he deserved it; and that he had taken upon him the obligation consenting to suffer the penalty if he violated it. In the two small volumes published by Elder Stearns, letters will be found from the most respectable and reliable Christian men. that fully sustain this statement, that the *adhering* fraternity, with very few exceptions, at that time, justified the murder of Morgan. In thus justifying that murder they, of course, admit that he violated his oath, and had truly published Freemasonry. I would quote these testimonies; but, as they can be read from the books themselves, I will not cumber these pages by copying them.

(*c.*) The credibility of these books is sustained by the express testimony of the seceding Masons, who, after hearing them read, ordered them printed.

(*d.*) The testimony of these books is further sustained by the report of a committee appointed at that time by the legislature of Rhode Island. That body appointed a committee, and gave them authority to arrest and examine Freemasons to ascertain whether the oaths published in these books were truly the oaths of Freemasons. This committee succeeded in bringing before them men that had taken the first ten degrees of Freemasonry. They put them on oath under the pains and penalties of perjury. In these circumstances they did not dare to deny it; but owned to the committee that they were the oaths taken by Freemasons. I said that they did not *dare* to deny it, because they were well aware that of seceding Masons hundreds and thousands might be obtained who would confront them and prove them guilty of perjury if they denied it.

I should have said that these Masons that were arrested, and that testified before this committee, were not *seceding*, but *adhering*, Masons. So that here for the first ten degrees of Freemasonry we have the admission *on oath* of *adhering* Masons that these books truly published their oaths. These facts may be learned from the records of the legislature, or from John Quincy Adams' letters to Mr. Livingston, who was at the head of the Masonic institution in the State of New York at that time.

(*e.*) The credibility of these books is further sustained by the implied admission of the two thousand lodges that suspended because their secrets were revealed, and because they were ashamed any longer to be known as sustaining the institution. These lodges, as I have before said, contained some forty-five thousand members. Now it should be particularly noted that, of all the seceding Masons in the United States, not one of them has ever, to my knowledge, denied that these books had truly revealed Masonry; while it is true that the five thousand who did not secede would never acknowledge that these books were credible. A worthy minister, who used to reside in this place, who has himself taken a great many degrees in Masonry, wrote to one of our citizens, a few months since, denouncing the institution in strong terms. He is a man who has traveled much among Freemasons for many years in various parts of the United States; and in that letter he affirmed that he had never known but one *adhering* Mason who would not deny, to those who did not know better, that those books had truly revealed Masonry. This is what might be expected.

(*f.*) The credibility of these books is further sustained by the published *individual* testimony of a great many men of unquestionable veracity—men standing high in the Christian ministry, and in church and state.

The books to which I have alluded contain very much of this kind of testimony.

But to all this testimony adhering Masons have objected. First, that the movement against Freemasonry was a *political* one. Answer: I have already said that by its having seized upon all the civil offices, and totally obstructing the course of justice, it was *forced* into politics by Masons themselves.

It was found that there was no other way than for the people to rise up and take the offices out of their hands by political action. At first there was no thought on the part of any one, so far as I could learn, that it would ever become a political question. But it was soon found that there was no other alternative.

But, again, it is said, Why should we receive the testimony of those men who have passed away, rather than the testimony of the living, thousands of whom now affirm that those books did not truly reveal Masonry?

To this I answer that these men are every one of them sworn to lie about it—expressly, or virtually. Observe, they must *conceal* as well as *never reveal* these secrets; therefore, as refusing to *deny* would be regarded as a virtual admission, they are sworn to make an impression amounting, morally, to a denial. At a recent conference of ministers and delegates from churches, a report was read by a committee previously appointed for that purpose, representing the true character of Freemasonry. I was not present, but am informed, by unquestionable authority, that after the report was read, a minister who was a Freemason represented the report as setting up a "*man of straw*" thereby intending to make the impression that the report was *not true.* But it was replied that the report may have exhibited "a man of straw," for such Freemasonry may be, but he was asked, is not the *report true?* To this question he refused to answer. Was this Christian honesty? At recess another minister, also a Freemason, in conversation spoke of the report as *trash*, but on being pressed with the question, "Is it not true?" he refused to answer. These cases illustrate their manner of disposing of this question. Many of them dare not *expressly* deny the truthfulness of those revelations, but they will so express themselves as to amount to a denial. They have numerous methods of doing this. They *intend* to *deceive*, manifestly for selfish reasons, and are therefore guilty of lying, and so they will find it held at the solemn judgment. If they adhere to their oaths, they are sworn to deny that these books truly reveal Masonry; and, therefore, their testimony is not to be received at all. But thousands of the *seceding* Masons still survive, and universally adhere to their testimony that those books did truly reveal Masonry.

But it is said that Masonry is *reformed*, and is not now what it was at that time.

Answer: First, this, then, is a virtual acknowledgment that at that time it was truly revealed. This is contradicting themselves

As long as they can, they deny that these books truly reveal it. But when forty-five thousand witnessess are summoned, among whom are a great many of the most valuable citizens of the United States, insomuch that they can have no face to deny that Masonry was revealed, as it then was, then we are told, "Oh! it is reformed; it is not what it was."

But, again, if they have reformed, the burden of proof is upon them. It is for them to show whether they have reformed out of it those things that rendered it so *odious* in a moral point of view, and so *dangerous* in a political point of view, as those books revealed it to be.

Again, their *authorities* do not *pretend* that it has been reformed. Their most recently published books take exactly the *opposite* ground, claiming that it is one and identical with what it was in the beginning; and that it neither has been nor can be changed in any of its essential principles or usages. They expressly require of their candidates to conform to all the *ancient* principles and usages of the institution. In another number I shall endeavor to set this question of reform at rest. It were premature to do so before we have examined the books in which it is revealed

I might sustain these assertions by copious extracts from their works, if it would not too much encumber this article. Let those who wish to know, get their books, and read them for themselves. If anything can be established by human testimony, it is forever beyond a doubt that Mr. Morgan, Elder Bernard, Mr. Richardson, and others that published Masonry, have published it substantially as it *was* and *is*.

I have already said that their secrets are never written by themselves. All their secrets are communicated orally. They take a great deal of pains to secure entire uniformity in regard to every word and sentiment which they teach. Each State has its lecturers, who go from lodge to lodge to teach and secure a uniformity as nearly perfect as possible.

And then there is a United States lecturer, who goes from State to State, to see that the grand lodges are all consistent with each other.

In spite, however, of all this painstaking and expense, slight verbal differences will exist among them. But these differences are only in words. The ideas are retained; but in some few instances they are expressed by different words, as we shall see when we come to examine the books themselves.

The fact is, that the great mass of young men who have joined them have been grossly deceived. Having been imposed upon, as I was imposed upon, they have been made to believe that the institution is a very different matter from what it really is.

We shall see hereafter how this imposition could be practiced upon them, and how it has been practiced upon them.

I would not be understood as denouncing the individuals composing the whole fraternity; for I am perfectly well persuaded that the great mass of young men who belong to the institution are laboring under a great delusion in regard to its real object, character, and tendency.

Lastly, it is inquired why we go to the *enemies* of Freemasonry for a knowledge of what it is, instead of getting our information from its friends. "Why not," they say, "allow us to speak for ourselves! We know what it is, and we can inform the public what it is; and why should you go to our enemies?" But what do Freemasons mean by asking such questions? Do they consider us *idiots?* Do they want to insult our intelligence by asking us why we don't get their secrets from *themselves?* Of course, as they well know, we cannot learn what the secrets of Masonry are from its friends and adherents, because they are under oath to give us no information about them. We are, therefore, under the necessity, if we would know what it is, of taking the testimony of those who know what it is by having taken its degrees, and have, from conscientious motives, renounced the institution. If they are its enemies, it is only in the sense that they regard the institution as not only unworthy of patronage, but as so wicked in a moral point of view, and so dangerous in a political point of view, that they feel constrained to reveal its secrets, and publicly to renounce it. These are the only men from whom we can possibly get any information of what Freemasonry is. It is absurd for *adhering* Masons to ask us why we do not allow *them* to teach us what it is; for *we* know, and *they* know, that they can do no such thing without violating their oaths and these oaths they still acknowledge to be binding upon them. Under this head I take the liberty to subjoin—

1. The testimony of the Albany Evening Journal Extra, of October 27, 1831. This article, as its date demonstrates, was written at the time of the investigation of the Morgan murder, and refers to facts too notorious to be denied:

"Since the public attention in this quarter

has been roused by recent events to the practical evils of Freemasonry, numerous inquiries are made for the means of information respecting the ridiculous ceremonies, the unlawful oaths, the dangerous obligations, and the blasphemous mockeries of this order. Although these have been from year to year, for the last five years, spread before the public, yet as our citizens here were indifferent to the subject, they avoided reading what was so profusely laid before them; and the consequence is, that now, when they begin to feel and think on this momentous matter, they find themselves in want of that information necessary to enable them to understand it. It shall be my purpose to supply the deficiency to some extent, by pointing out the sources of full and extensive knowledge, and by presenting as briefly as possible, the prominent features in the character of Freemasonry. It has become a question of such engrossing interest, that every man should desire to be informed, and every citizen who is called upon to act in reference to it in his capacity as AN ELECTOR, is bound by the highest duties of patriotism to act understandingly.

"The first revelation of Masonry in this country was made by William Morgan. In 1826, he published a pamphlet, entitled 'Illustiations in Masonry,' in which the ceremonies of initiation and the obligations of the three first degrees were disclosed. For this publication he was kidnapped and forcibly carried away from a wife and two children, and was murdered by being drowned in the Niagara River. This was done by Freemasons. Thus he has sealed the truth of his revelations by sacrificing his own life, and the Freemasons established their accuracy incontrovertibly by the punishment they inflicted on him. For according to their own bloody code, he could not have incurred the penalty of death, if he had not revealed their *secrets*. In February, 1828, a convention of seceding Masons was held at Le Roy, in the County of Genesee, composed of some thirty or forty of the most respectable citizens. They published a declaration to the world under their signatures, in which they declared the revelations of William Morgan to be strictly true and perfectly accurate. Under the same responsibility they also published the oaths and obligations of the higher orders. In the course of the same year, Elder Bernard, a Baptist clergyman of good character, and who was a distinguished Mason, published a work, entitled 'Light on Masonry,' in which the ceremonies, oaths and mummeries of the order are given at full length. In 1829, on the trial of Elihu Mather, in Orleans County, the obligations of the three first degrees and of a Royal Arch Mason, were proved, at a Circuit Court held by Judge Gardiner, by the testimony of three seceding Masons and one adhering Mason. In obedience to a resolution of the Senate of New York, Judge Gardiner reported this evidence, and it was printed by order of the Senate. In 1830, on a trial in Rhode Island, the same obligations were proved in open court, and the trial was published at large in the newspapers. In 1831, on the trial of H. C. Witherell, at New Berlin, in Chenango County, the same obligations were proved by the oaths of three adhering Masons, among whom was General Welch, the sheriff of the county. In the year 1830, Avery Allyn, a regular Knight Templar, published a book, called the 'Ritual of Freemasonry,' in which the ceremonies of initiation, the lectures, oaths and mummeries of *thirty-one* degrees are fully exhibited. Thousands of Masons individually have, under their names in the public papers, declared these publications of Bernard and Allyn to be strictly accurate. These books may be found 'n our bookstores."

2. I next subjoin a tract, made up of "The Petition to the Legislature of Connecticut.' against extra-judicial oaths, with an abstract

of the evidence, and the report of the Committee to whom the subject was referred. Published in 1834:

*To the Honorable General Assembly of the State of Connecticut, to be holden at Hartford, on the first Wednesday of May, A. D. 1833:*

THE Petitioners, inhabitants of said State, respectfully request the attention of your Honorable body to the expediency of some legal provision to prevent the administration of oaths in all cases not authorized by law. It may justly be required of the Petitioners, before a compliance can be expected with this request, that a case should be made out requiring such Legislative provision; and your Petitioners confidently trust that satisfactory grounds for this application will be found to exist in the oaths which are administered in Masonic Lodges.

The disclosures which have been recently made by the seceding Masons of the secret proceedings of those Lodges fully prove that the Institution of Freemasonry consists of numerous degress which may be increased to an unlimited extent, and that an oath of an extraordinary character is administered at the entrance of every degree. Your Petitioners would not trespass upon the principles of decorum by an unnecessary recital of all these horrid imprecations, but justice to the cause they have espoused compels them to exhibit the following specimens, which are selected from the oaths administered in the different degrees: The Entered Apprentice Mason swears, "I will always hail, ever conceal, and never reveal any part or parts, art or arts, point or points of the secrets, arts, and mysteries of Ancient Freemasonry which I have received, am about to receive, or may hereafter be instructed in;" "without the least equivocation, mental reservation, or self-evasion of mind in me whatever, binding myself under no less penalty than to have my throat cut across, my tongue torn out by the roots, and my body buried in the rough sands of the sea." The Master Mason swears, "I will obey all regular signs, summonses, or tokens, given, handed, sent, or thrown to me from the hand of a brother Master Mason;" "a Master Mason's secrets, given to me in charge as such, and I knowing them to be such, shall remain as secure and inviolable in my breast as in his own, when communicated to me, *murder and treason excepted*, and they left to my own election." The Royal Arch Mason swears, "I will aid and assist a companion Royal Arch Mason when engaged in any difficulty; and espouse his cause so far as to extricate him from the same, if in my power, whether he be right or wrong." "A Companion Royal Arch Mason's secrets, given me in charge as such, and 1 knowing them to be such, shall remain as secure and inviolable in my breast as in his own, *without exception.*" The following obligations are contained in the oath of the Holy Thrice Illustrious order of the Cross, Knights, or Kadosh, etc.: "I swear to put confidence unlimited in every illustrious brother of the Cross as a true and worthy follower of the blessed Jesus;" "I swear to look on his enemies as my enemies, his friends as my friends, and to stand forth to mete out tender kindness or vengeance accordingly." "I solemnly swear, in the presence of Almighty God, that I will revenge the assassination of our worthy Master Hiram Abiff, not only on his murderers, but also on all who may betray the secrets of this degree." "I swear to take revenge on the traitors of Masonry."

It can not be necessary for your Petitioners to enter upon a formal argument in order to satisfy this enlightened Assembly that oaths like the foregoing ought not to be administered. The guarded and redundant language in which they are expressed, and the barbarous and abhorrent penalties annexed to them, were evidently designed to impose upon the mind of the candidate the necessity of entire and universal obedience to their requirements. They purport to be the injunctions of supreme power, and claim supremacy over every obligation, human or divine. In this light they were regarded and acted upon by Masons of high standing and character who were concerned in the late Masonic murder committed in the State of New York, or connected with the trials which sprang from it, and in this construction these Masons were justified and upheld by the Grand Chapter and Grand Lodge of that State. Such obligations are obviously inconsistent with our allegiance to the State, and the obedience which is required by our Maker, and with those fundamental principles which constitute the basis and the cement of civil and of religious communities. The Masonic oaths lead directly to the sacrifice of duties and the commission of crimes; they cherish a feeling of selfishness and of savage revenge, instead of the spirit of the Gospel, and are the ground-work of an insidious attempt to effect the entire overthrow of our holy religion.

It is for these reasons that your Petitioners respectfully request your Honors, by a suitable legal provision, to prohibit the administration of oaths not authorized by law; and they, as in duty bound, will ever pray.

The foregoing was the petition of about fourteen hundred citizens of the State of Connecticut, and was presented to the Legislature at their session in May, 1833. By the House of Representatives it was referred to a select committee, who, having given notice of the time and place of their meeting, entered into an investigation of the subject. The sittings of the committee were open to the public, and every person who wished to hear the proceedings could attend, if he chose. Three witnesses were presented by the Petitioners, viz.: Mr. Hanks, of New York, and Messrs. Welch and Hatch, of this State, by whom they expected to substantiate the facts as set forth in the petition. In giving his testimony, Mr. Hanks read the several oaths, etc., as published in Allyn's Ritual, beginning with that of the Entered Apprentice, and pointing out, as he proceeded, any discrepancies or variations which he had practiced or known. He had taken, administered, or seen administered, the oaths, etc., in four different States of the Union viz.: New York, Pennsylvania, Virginia, and Ohio—had taken, himself, many degrees, and testified from personal knowledge. The testimony of Mr. Hanks was full, explicit, and particular on the first seven degrees of Masonry, and his statements were supported by those of Messrs. Welch and Hatch, as far as their experience extended.

Among the facts proved by the testimony were the following, viz.: that Freemasonry, with its oaths and penalties, is substantially the same everywhere—that the variations are slight, and, in most instances, merely verbal, and such as have resulted from unwritten or traditionary communication—that the oaths and penalties of the first seven degrees are revealed to the world and correctly published by Mr. Allyn in his Ritual, and by others—that they are so administered in the lodges, and are to be understood according to the plain, literal import of the terms in which they are expressed, and as they have been explained by seceding Masons generally—that the declaration of the Massachusetts and Connecticut adhering Masons can not be made, or signed understandingly, in consistence with truth—that in the Royal Arch oath the terms "murder and treason not excepted" are sometimes used; sometimes the expression "in all cases whatsoever," or "in all cases without exception." Some other verbal alterations were noticed, which need not be detailed here. It appeared, also, from the statements of the witnesses, that the proportion of funds disposed of for charitable purposes is extremely small, while the lodges are scenes of extravagant mirth and bacchanalian revelry, and the admission, passing, and raising of candidates occasions of much indecent sport and ridiculous merriment, accompanied with mock murders, feigned discoveries, and profane and blasphemous ceremonies and representations.

From the evidence before them the committee came to the conclusions expressed in the following

## REPORT.

*To the Honorable General Assembly of the State of Connecticut now in Session:*

The committee to whom was referred the petition of Gaius Lyman and others beg leave respectfully to report that we have had the same under consideration, and inquired, by legal evidence, into the truth of the matters therein set forth, and are of the opinion that the same have been substantially proved, and are true. The committee, at the commencement of the investigation, adopted the rule, and made known the same to the petitioners, that we should attend to no evidence except such as, in our opinion, would be admissible in a court of law. The petitioners accordingly summoned before us sundry witnesses who, for aught we knew or could discover to the contrary, were men of respectability and intelligence, and upon their testimony, and upon *that alone*, have we come to our present result. It was proved by these witnesses that oaths similar in character (and some of them identical in phraseology) to those set forth in the petition had been, in their presence and within their hearing, repeatedly administered in this State. The committee believe the administration of such oaths to be highly improper, and that the same should be prohibited by legal enactment. Our reasons for this opinion are:

1. Because they are unauthorized by law.
2. Because they bind the person to whom they are administered to disregard and violate the law.
3. Because they are, in their natural tendency, subversive of public morals and blasphemous.
4. Because the penalties attached to the breach of them are such as are entirely unknown to our law, and are forbidden both by the Constitution of the United States and by the Constitution of this State.

First, then, these oaths are not authorized

by law. In our code of statute law we have an act which points out the cases in which oaths shall or may be administered, and prescribes their several forms. In this act we find no such oaths. Indeed, we find, upon examination of this code, that although extra judicial oaths are nowhere expressly prohibited, their unlawfulness is throughout clearly implied. And the implication is no less clear, that no persons, except those expressly authorized by law, may rightfully administer oaths. The committee would barely refer to a number of those acts in which particular persons are, on particular occasions and for particular purposes, authorized to administer oaths. In the act relative to insolvency, the commissioners are expressly authorized to administer an oath to the insolvent debtor. In the act relative to surveyors, the surveyors are authorized to administer an oath to the chainmen. In the act relating to oaths, passed in 1822, Clerks of the Senate and House of Representatives, and the Chairmen of Committees are, during the session of the Legislature, authorized to administer oaths. There are other acts of the same nature, to which it can not be necessary particularly to refer. The inference, as we think plainly deducible from these acts, is, that *all* persons have not the right to administer oaths·

and that those oaths only which the law prescribes may be lawfully administered. And we need only ask this Honorable Body whether the public sense of propriety would not be shocked at witnessing, in open daylight, the administration of an oath by a person not by law authorized, and in a case not by law provided for. For instance, suppose a clergyman, upon the admission of a member into his church, should require him to kneel down, place his hand upon the Bible, and then solemnly swear that he would observe all the rules and regulations of that church, upon no less penalty than to have his throat cut across, his tongue torn out by the roots, and his body buried in the rough sands of the sea; would not an involuntary shudder pervade the whole community at such a horrid exhibition; and would not our first impression be that this clergyman had violated the law, and that he ought forthwith to be prosecuted? And yet we may search our statute book in vain for any penal enactment that would reach this case. Again, suppose that any one of the charitable and benevolent societies of the present day should, on the admission of a member, compel him to swear by the ever-living God that he would obey all the laws of the society "upon no less penalty than to have his left breast torn open, his heart and vitals taken therefrom, thrown over his left shoulder, and carried into the valley of Jehoshaphat, there to become a prey to the wild beasts of the field and the vultures of the air." And, moreover, suppose this oath to be administered by some one not by law authorized to administer *any* oath. We need scarcely ask whether an insulted community would not, under a sense that their laws had been wantonly trampled upon, call aloud, and with earnestness, upon the ministers of justice to punish such awful and disgusting profanity. And yet the ministers of justice could afford them no aid, inasmuch as the law has not, on this subject, clothed them with any authority.

Secondly. We object to the administration of oaths like those set forth in the petition, because they bind the person receiving them to disregard and violate the law. In one of the oaths, for instance, the person receiving it swears that he will assist a companion of a certain degree, so far as to extricate him from difficulty, whether he be right or wrong. He also swears that he will keep the secrets of a companion of a certain degree *without exception*, or as the witnesses testified they had heard it administered, "murder and treason not excepted." Now, the committee believe it to be morally wrong, as well as inconsistent with our allegiance to the government under which we live, and a direct violation of the law, to keep secret the commission of any great and flagrant offense against the government. He who conceals treason is himself guilty of misprision of treason. He who conceals murder is himself (in some cases at least) a murderer.

Thirdly. We consider the administration of extra-judicial oaths, especially such as are set forth in said petition, improper, because in their tendency they are opposed to sound morals and are blasphemous. The obligation to assist another so far as to extricate him from difficulty, whether he be right or wrong, and to conceal another's secrets, even though those secrets should involve the highest and most enormous crimes, is most assuredly opposed to the spirit of the Gospel, and to the pure system of morality therein inculcated. And to call upon the great and awful name of Jehovah to give sanction to such obligations is, in our opinion, the hight of blasphemy.

Fourthly. We believe such oaths to be improper, because the penalties attached to them are such as are unknown to our law, and are opposed both to the Constitution of the United States and to the Constitution of this State. If the breach of those oaths constitute the crime of perjury, then, in our opinion, such breach should be punished as perjury in other cases is punished. By our law every person who shall commit perjury, and shall be thereof duly convicted, shall suffer imprisonment in the Connecticut State Prison not less than two nor more than five years; and this is the extent of the pains and penalties which the humanity of our law will suffer to be inflicted upon him. But to the violation of the oaths above referred to is annexed a great variety of most cruel and inhuman punishments, such as are not known in the criminal codes of any civilized nation on the earth. Among them are the tearing out of the tongue, or splitting it from tip to roots—the cutting of the throat across from ear to ear—the tearing out of the heart and vitals, and exposing them to be destroyed by wild beasts and birds of prey, etc. These penalties we believe to be forbidden by the tenth article of the amendments of the Constitution of the United States, which prohibits the infliction of all cruel and unusual punishments; and by the tenth section of the first article of the Constitution of this State, which declares that "No person shall be arrested, detained, or punished, except in cases clearly warranted by law." For these and for various other reasons which must be obvious to the good sense of this Honorable Body, we are of the opinion that the prayer of the petition ought to be granted, and we would, therefore, recommend the passage of the accompanying Bill for a public Act. All of which is respectfully submitted. Signed per order,

THOMAS BACKUS, *Chairman.*

3. I introduce the published renunciation of Freemasonry by Jarvis F. Hanks, of New York, 1829, and of Calvin Hatch, published 1831 Also, the published renunciation of Henry Fish, Edwin Chapman, and Bliss Welch, 1830. These are found on the cover of the tract, and are only specimens of a multitude of similar renunciations published in various books and journals.

## RENUNCIATION.

"*To the Editor of the Anti-Masonic Beacon.*

"SIR: The time has come when I feel constrained, from a sense of duty to God, my neighbor, and myself, to make void my allegiance to the Masonic Institution. In thus taking leave of Freemasonry, I am not sensible of the least hostility to Masons; but act under a solemn conviction that Masonry is a wicked imposture, a refuge of lies, a substitute for the Gospel of Christ; that it is contrary to the laws of God and our country, and superior to either, in the estimation of its disciples; and lastly, that it is the most powerful and successful engine ever employed by the devil to destroy the souls of men.

"I was initiated into Masonry in 1821, and have taken eighteen degrees. My motives were curiosity and the expectation of personal advantage, while, at the same time, I was dishonest enough to profess that disinterested benevolence to my fellow-men was my object. I have been intrusted with the highest offices in the gift of a Lodge and Chapter, viz.: Worshipful Master and Most Excellent High Priest, which I acknowledge, at that time, I considered very flattering distinctions. I approved of the abduction of William Morgan as a just act of Masonry, and had I been called upon to assist, should, under the opinions I then held, have felt bound to *attend the summons and obey it.* I remained in favor of the Institution several months after the abduction of Morgan.

"I was convinced of the evil and folly of Masonry from an inquiry instituted in my own mind, which I was determined should be conducted privately, candidly, impartially, and, if possible, without prejudice. Under the scrutiny of the investigation I brought the Law of God contained in the Old and New Testaments, the laws of our country, the Masonic oaths (so many as I have taken), Masonic professions, and Masonic practice. I then resolved not to be influenced by the fear or favor of man, who can only '*kill the body, and after that has no more that he can do,* but by the fear of God, '*who, after he hath killed, hath power to cast into hell.*' (Luke xii. 4, 5.) I feel assured that any Mason, or any man, taking the same course, must arrive at the same conclusion.     Yours,     JARVIS F. HANKS.

"NEW YORK, *February* 13, 1829."

## CALVIN HATCH'S RENUNCIATION OF FREEMASONRY.

"*To the Church of Christ in Farmington:*

"BRETHREN: Impressed with a sense of duty, I would solicit your attention, while I make the following statement of facts. Soon after I arrived at the age of twenty-one years I was induced (principally from curiosity) to become a Freemason; and before I was twenty-two, I advanced to the third, and soon after to the fourth degree of the then *hidden mysteries* of that Institution, and remained a tolerably regular attendant upon its stated meetings, until February, 1819; since which I have never attended any of its meetings, though often requested.

"Hoodwinked to the principles of the Institution, I felt that, as a professed follower of the Lord Jesus Christ, it was not profitable to spend my time in the lodge-room.

"Another fact I wish to notice: that for three years I was accustomed to hear prayers offered at the lodge by a man who was considered an infidel; which, to my mind, was utterly revolting.

"Within about a year my attention has been particularly called to this subject. At first, I felt that the Institution could not be bad, except by being in the hands of bad men. I satisfied myself that my withdrawment from the lodge, while Masonry was in good repute, spoke a language which could not be misunderstood; and still, I confess I felt some veneration for the Institution, on account of its beneficence n relieving its afflicted members.

"Early last spring I became satisfied that one of our citizens had fallen a sacrifice to Masonic vengeance; yet, whether the Institution could be charged with it, was with me a question. I found that it was thus charged by those opposed to the Institution, and I hastily and rashly resolved to read no more upon the subject, because I considered the charge unjust. In the course of the last summer I had many misgivings for this decision, which closed every avenue to information. Knowing that many of my Christian brethren were grieved that any professor of the religion of Christ should remain even a nominal member of a society, the principles of which they believed were anti-christian, and opposed to the best interests of our country.

"Feeling that some deference was due to their judgment, I, early in the fall, with prayerfulness, divesting myself of all prejudice, took up the subject for investigating the principles, and sought information through the press, and soon became satisfied that I had a duty to perform which I had long neglected; and in December last, without consulting anyone, came to the conclusion that nothing short of absolving myself from all connection with the Masonic Fraternity, and from all its obligations, would be answerable to my duty as a citizen and a member of the church of Christ. Since that time I have read the proceedings of the United States Anti-Masonic Convention, disclosing facts before unknown to me, and am of the opinion that it is the bounden duty of every professor of religion who feels bound in the least by Masonic obligations to read the doings of that convention, with prayerfulness and without prejudice, before he decides upon the path of duty.

"I feel that some acknowledgments are due from me to those brethren who have been grieved by my dilatoriness upon a subject so plain and a duty so clear. And if I have thus offended any of my brethren, I pray them to forgive; and however great my sin has been, I trust I have forgiveness of my God.

"I can not dismiss the subject without beseeching my Christian brethren who remain as I have done, to examine and decide, as in the presence of God, without delay; for what we do must be done quicky. CALVIN HATCH.

"FARMINGTON, *February* 3, 1831."

---

COPY OF MY RENUNCIATION SENT BY MAIL TO NEW MILFORD, FEBRUARY 3, 1831.

"*To the Officers of St. Peter's Lodge, New Milford, State of Connecticut:*

"GENTLEMEN: For more than twenty years I have been a member of your lodge; and now, from a conviction that it is my duty as a citizen and a professed follower of our blessed Savior no longer to remain, even as I have been for the last twelve years, a nominal member of a society whose principles are opposed to the best interests of our country, and whose rites are, many of them, not only immoral, but a profanation of Scripture, and, consequently opposed to the religion of the Gospel, I do therefore, absolve myself from all its obligations whatever.     CALVIN HATCH.

"FARMINGTON, *December* 25, 1830."

## RENUNCIATION.

"Having been initiated some years since in the mysteries of Freemasonry, but without finding any of those advantages which were so bountifully promised by the Fraternity, and now being fully convinced that the Institution is corrupt to the very core, and used to promote ends tending to subvert our free institutions, we deem it our duty publicly to renounce all obligations to the 'Craft,' believing ourselves to be freed from its oaths, inasmuch as no man can bind himself to do anything contrary to the allegiance he owes to his country, or the duties he owes to his Maker.

"HENRY FISH, Salisbury, Master Mason
"EDWIN CHAPMAN, Windsor, M. Mason
"BLISS WELCH, Chatham, Royal Arch.
"Dated at HARTFORD, *Feb.* 4 1830."

## CHAPTER V.

## EXAMINATION OF THE BOOKS REVEALING FREEMASONRY.

HAVING established the fact that Bernard in his "Light on Masonry," William Morgan, Allyn, Richardson, and others, all of whom substantially agree, have truly revealed Freemasonry as it was at that time, I will now enter upon an examination of some of these books, assuming as I must, or abandon all idea that any thing can ever be proved by human testimony, that they contain a veritable revelation of Freemasonry.

After I have examined these books, and learned and shown what Freemasonry was at their date, I shall consider the question of its having undergone any material change since that date, and also whether it can be so changed as to be an innocent institution and still retain the distinguishing characteristics of Freemasonry.

That I may do no injustice to any one. I shall not hold Masons responsible for oaths and degrees which are above and beyond them and which they have not taken and of which they have no knowledge. The question of their moral and responsible relation to the institution, *as a whole*, will receive notice in another place. At present I shall hold Masons responsible for those oaths, principles, teachings and degrees of which they have knowledge.

In these numbers I need only to notice a few points in the oaths of Masons, and I recommend all persons to obtain the books in which their oaths, ceremonies, and secrets are fully revealed. The first of their oaths is that of an Entered Apprentice. These oaths are administered in the following manner: The candidate stands on his knees, with his hands on the Holy Bible. The Worshipful Master pronounces the oath in short sentences, and the candidate repeats after him. The oath of the Entered Apprentice is as follows: " I, A. B., of my own free will and accord, in presence of Almighty God and this worshipful lodge of Free and Accepted Masons, dedicated to God and held forth to the holy order of St. John, do hereby and hereon most sincerely promise and swear, that I will always hail. ever conceal, and never reveal any part or parts, art or arts, point or points of the secrets, arts, and mysteries of ancient Freemasonry, which I have received, am about to receive, or may hereafter be instructed in, to any person or persons in the known world, except it be a true and lawful brother Mason, or within the body of a just and lawfully constituted lodge of such; and not unto him or unto them whom I shall hear so to be, but unto him and them only whom I shall find so to be after strict trial and due examination, or lawful information.

"Furthermore, do I promise and swear, that I will not write, print, stamp, stain, hew, cut, carve, indent, paint, or engrave it on anything movable or immovable under the whole canopy of Heaven, whereby or whereon the least letter, figure, character, mark, stain, shadow, or resemblance may become legible or intelligible to myself or to any other person in the known world, whereby the secrets of Masonry may be unlawfully obtained through my unworthiness. To all of which I do most solemnly and sincerely promise and swear, without the least equivocation, mental reservation, or self-evasion of mind in me whatever; binding myself under no less penalty than to have my throat cut across, my tongue torn out by the roots, and my body buried in the rough sands of the sea at ow-water mark, where the tide ebbs and flows twice in twenty-four hours. So help me God.

and keep me steadfast in the due performance of the same."—*Light on Masonry*, 8*th edition*, *page* 27.

Upon this oath I remark:

1. That the administration and taking of it are in direct violation of both the law and gospel of God. Jesus prohibits the taking of oaths. Mat. V. 34. "But I say unto you swear not at all." It is generally conceded that He intended *only* to forbid the taking of extra *judicial oaths*. That He did formally and positively forbid the taking, and of course the administering, of all oaths not regularly administered for judicial and governmental purposes, is, I believe, universally admitted. Here then we find that in the first step in Freemasonry the express command of Christ is set at nought.

2. The administration and taking of this oath is a taking of the name of God in vain and is therefore an awful profanity. Exod. xx: 7: "Thou shalt not take the name of the Lord thy God in vain: for the Lord will not hold him guiltless that taketh his name in vain." Professing Christian Freemasons, do you hear and remember this, and are you aware that in taking or administering this oath you take the name of God in vain and that He will not hold you guiltless? Do you also remember that

whenever you are present aiding, abetting, and consenting to the administering, and taking of this or any other Masonic oath you are guilty of violating the express command of Christ above quoted, and also the express prohibition of the lawgiver at Sinai? And yet you can see nothing unchristian in Freemasonry.

3. This oath pledges the candidate to keep whatever secrets they may communicate to him. But, for aught he knows, it may be unlawful to keep them. This oath is a snare to his soul. It must be wicked to thus commit himself on oath. The spirit of God's word forbids it.

4. The administrator of this oath had just assured the candidate that there was nothing in it inconsistent with his duty to God or to man. How is it, professed Christian, that you did not remember that you had no right to take an oath at all under such circumstances and for such reasons. Why did you not inquire of the Master by what authority he was about to administer an oath, and by what authority he expected and required you to take it? Why did you not ask him if God would hold him guiltless if he administered an oath in His name, and you guiltless if you took the oath. And when you have seen this or any other Masonic oath administered why have you

not rebuked the violation of God's law and left the lodge ?

5. Why did the Master assure the candidate that there was nothing in the oath contrary to his obligations to God or man, and then instantly proceed to violate the laws of both God and man and to require of the candidate the same violation of law, human and divine?

6. The penalty for violating this oath is monstrous, barbarous, savage, and is utterly repugnant to all laws of morality, religion or decency. Binding myself "under no less a penalty than to have my throat cut across, my tongue torn out by the roots, and my body buried in the sands of the sea at low-water mark, etc." Now, has any man a right to incur such a penalty as this?

I say again: such a penalty is savage, barbarous, unchristian, inhuman, abominable. It should be here remarked that in this oath is really found the *virus* of all that follows in Freemasonry. The candidate is sworn to keep secret everything that *is to be revealed to him in Freemasonry* of *which as yet* he *knows absolutely nothing.* This is frequently repeated in the obligations that follow.

It will be observed that the candidate says, "to all of which I do solemnly and sincerely promise and swear, without the least equivoce tion, mental reservation, or self-evasion of mind in me, whatever." Richardson, who published the Freemason's Monitor in 1860, on the 4th page of his preface, says of Masonry: "The oaths and obligations were then undoubtedly binding (that is when Freemasonry was first established), not only for the protection of the members but for the preservation of the very imperfect arts and sciences of that period. To suppose these oaths mean anything now is simply absurd." What! How is this compatible with what is said in this first oath of Masonry, and hence binding through every degree of Masonry. "ALL THIS, I MOST SOLEMNLY AND SINCERELY PROMISE AND SWEAR, WITHOUT THE LEAST EQUIVOCATION, MENTAL RESERVATION, OR SELF-EVASION OF MIND IN ME WHATEVER." And now we are told by one of the highest Masonic authorities, that, to suppose that Masonic oaths *mean* anything in these days, is simply absurd. THEN, SURELY THEY ARE BLASPHEMY.

## CHAPTER VI.

## MASTER S DEGREE.

I PASS over the second degree of Masonry, the oath of which, in substance is similar to that in the first, and in this number will consider the oath, or obligation of a Master Mason. I do not notice the ridiculous manner in which the candidate for the different degrees, is dressed and conducted into the lodge. The scenes through which they pass, are most humiliating and ridiculous, and cannot fail to be so regarded by all who will read the books in which they are described. I quote from the eighth edition of "Light on Masonry," by Elder David Bernard, published by W. J. Shuey, Dayton, Ohio. The obligation of the Master's degree will be found on the seventy-third and seventy-fourth pages of this work, and is as follows: "I, A. B., of my own free will and accord, in the presence of Almighty God, and this worshipful Lodge of Master Masons, erected to God, and dedicated to the holy order of St. John, do hereby and hereon, most solemnly and sincerely promise and swear, *in addition to my former obligations*, that I will not give the degree of Master Mason to any one of an inferior degree, nor to any one in the known world, except it be to a true and lawful brother or brethren Master Mason, or within the body of a just and lawfully constituted lodge of such; and not unto him nor unto them whom I shall hear so to be, but unto him and them only whom I shall find so to be, after strict trial and due examination, or lawful information received. Furthermore, do I promise and swear, that I will not give the Master's word which I shall hereafter receive neither in the lodge nor out of it, except it be on the five points of fellowship, and then not above my breath. Furthermore, do I promise and swear, that I will not give the grand hailing sign of distress, except I am in real distress, or for the benefit of the craft when at work; or should I ever see that sign given, or hear the word accompanying it and the person who gave it, appearing to be in distress, I will fly to his relief at the risk of my life, should there be a greater probability of saving his life than of losing my own. Furthermore, do I promise and swear that I will not wrong this lodge, nor a brother of this degree, to the value of one cent knowingly, myself, nor suffer it to be done by others, if in my power to prevent. Furthermore, do I promise and swear, that I will not be at the initiating, passing, and raising, a candidate at one communication, without a regular dispensation from the Grand Lodge for the same. Furthermore, do I promise and swear, that I will not be at the initiating, passing, or raising a candidate in a clandestine lodge, I knowing it to be such. Furthermore, do I promise and swear, that I will not be at the initiating of an old man in dotage, a young man in nonage, an atheist, irreligious libertine, idiot, madman, hermaphrodite, nor woman Furthermore, do I promise and swear, that I will not speak evil of a brother Master Mason, neither behind his back, nor before his face, but will apprise him of all approaching danger if in my power. Furthermore, do I promise and swear, that I will not violate the chastity of a Master Mason's wife, mother, sister, or daughter, I knowing them to be such, nor suffer it to be done by others, if in my power to prevent it. Furthermore, do I promise and swear, that I will support the constitution of the Grand Lodge of the State of ———, under which this lodge is held, and conform to all the by-laws, rules and regulations of this, or any other lodge, of which I may at any time hereafter become a member. Furthermore, do I promise and swear, that I will obey all regular signs, summons, or tokens, given, handed, sent, or thrown to me, from the hand of another brother Master Mason, or from the body of a just and lawfully constituted lodge of such, provided it be within the length of my cable tow. Furthermore, do I promise and swear, that a Master Mason's secrets, given to me in charge as such, and I knowing them to be such, shall remain as secure and inviolable in my breast as in his own, murder and treason excepted, and they left to my own election. Furthermore, do I promise and swear, that I will go on a Master Mason's errand whenever required, even should I have to go barefoot and bareheaded, if within the length of my cable tow. Furthermore, do I promise and swear, that I will always remember a brother Master Mason when on my knees, offering up my devotions to Almighty God. Furthermore, do I promise and swear, that I will be aiding and assisting all poor, indigent Master Masons, their wives and orphans, wheresoever disposed around the globe, as far as in my power without injuring myself or family materially. Furthermore, do I promise and swear, that if any part of this solemn oath or obligation be omitted at this time that I will hold myself amenable thereto, whenever in formed. To all which I do most solemnly promise and swear, with a fixed and steady purpose of mind in me, to keep and perform the same, binding myself under no less penalty than to have my body severed in two in the midst, and divided to the north and south, my bowels burnt to ashes in the center and the ashes scattered before the four winds of heaven, that there might not the least track or trace of remembrance remain among men and Masons of so vile and perjured a wretch as I should be, were I ever to prove willfully guilty of violating *any part* of this my solemn oath or obligation of a Master Mason. So help me God, and keep me steadfast in the due performance of the same."

Upon this oath I remark:

1. The first sentence is both profane and false. The Master instructs the kneeling candidate with his hand on God's Holy Word to affirm, and the candidate does affirm that the lodge in which he is kneeling is erected to God and dedicated to the holy order of St. John. Remember this is said in and of every Master Masons' lodge. But is this true? No. indeed it is mere mockery. The words are a mere profane form. Does not every Freemason know this?

2. *This*, and all the following oaths of Ma-

sonry, are administered and taken as *additions* to all the previous oaths which the candidate has taken. (See the oath.) All that is wicked and profane in the former oaths is indorsed and reaffirmed in this and in every succeeding oath. Thus Freemasons proceed to pile oath upon oath in a manner most shocking and revolting. And is this a Christian institution? Is this obedience to Him who has said "swear not at all?"

3. The grand hailing sign of distress mentioned in this oath, consists in raising both hands to heaven in the attitude of supplication. The words accompanying this sign are, "*O Lord, my God, is there no help for the widow's son?*" The candidate is told by the Master that this attitude was taken and these words were used by Solomon when he was informed of the murder of Hiram Abiff. Of this, "Light on Masonry" will give the reader full information. This whole story of the murder of Hiram Abiff is a profane falsehood, as I shall more fully show in another place. Hiram Abiff was never murdered. Solomon never gave any such sign, or uttered any such words. The whole story is false; both the grand hailing sign of distress, and the accompanying words, are a profane mockery, and an insult to God. But what is the thing promised in this part of

a Master Mason's oath? Observe, the candidate swears, 'should I ever see that sign given, or hear the word accompanying it, and the person who gave it, appearing to be in distress, I will fly to his relief at the risk of my life, should there be a greater probability of saving his life than of losing my own." Observe, it matters not what is the cause of the distress in which a Master Mason may be—if he has committed a crime, and is likely to be arrested, or has been arrested; if he is imprisoned, or likely to be imprisoned; if he is on trial in a court of justice and likely to be convicted, and a Master Mason is on the bench as a judge, or on the jury or called as a witness; or is a Master Mason a sheriff and has the prisoner in custody; or is he a constable, having charge of the jury to whom the case is to be submitted; or is he a prosecuting attorney, appointed by the government to prosecute him for his crime, and secure his conviction—in any of these cases, the prisoner giving the grand hailing sign of distress, binds, by a most solemn oath, the judge, jurymen, sheriff, constable, witness, attorney, if a Master Mason, to seek to release him, at the hazard of his life. All who are acquainted with the practical results of this section of the Master's oath, as they appeared in the investigations connected with the murder of William

Morgan, are aware that Master Masons kept this oath inviolate, when efforts were made to convict the kidnappers and murderers, insomuch that it was found impossible to execute the laws. Cases are reported as having repeatedly occurred in the administration of justice, where this hailing sign of distress has prevailed to rescue the guilty from the hand of justice. In another part of this oath, you will observe, the candidate swears, that he will apprise a brother Master Mason of approaching danger, if within his power. This binds a Master Mason to give a criminal notice, if he understands that he is about to be arrested. If the sheriff has a writ for the arrest of a brother Master Mason, this oath lays him under an obligation not to arrest him, but to give him notice, that if he does not keep out of the way, he shall be obliged to arrest him. If the magistrate who issued the writ is a Master Mason, his oath obliges him to give the criminal Master Mason warning, so that he may evade the execution of the writ. Reader, get and read the pamphlet published by Judge Whitney, of Belvidere, Illinois. It can be had, I believe, at the bookstores in this town. This pamphlet will give you an acconnt of the trial of Judge Whitney, who was Master of a lodge, before the Grand Lodge of Illinois. It will show you how completely this oath may prevail to obstruct the whole course of justice, and render the execution of the law impossible. If a Master Mason is suspected of a crime, and his case comes before a justice of the peace who is a Master Mason, or before a grand jury upon which there is a Master Mason, or before a court or petit jury in which are Master Masons, if they keep inviolate their oath, it is impossible to reach the execution of the law. Furthermore, if there be Master Masons in the community, who hear of the guilt and danger of a brother Master Mason, they are sworn to give him warning. It is no doubt for this reason, that Masons try to secure amongst themselves all the offices connected with the administration of justice. At the time of the murder of Morgan, it was found that to such an extent were these offices in the hands of Freemasons that the courts were entirely impotent. I quote the following from "Stearns' Letters on Freemasonry," page 127: "In speaking of the murder of William Morgan, of the justice of it, and of the impossibility of punishing his murderers, a justice of the peace in Middlebury, a sober, respectable man, and a Mason, said, 'that a man had a *right* to pledge his life,' and then observed: 'What can you do? What can a rat do with a lion? Who are you judges? who are your sheriffs? and who will be your jurymen?'" It is perfectly plain that if Freemasons mean anything by this oath, as they have given frequent evidence that they do, this obligation must be an effectual bar to the administration of justice wherever Freemasons are numerous. No wonder, therefore, that dishonest men among them are very anxious greatly to multiply their numbers. In the days of William Morgan, they had so multiplied their numbers that it was found impossible, and in these days Freemasons have become so numerous, that in many places it *will* be found impossible to execute the criminal laws. Even in commercial transactions where Freemasons are parties to a suit, it will be found impossible to secure the ends of justice Let not Freemasons complain of this assertion

4. You will observe that in this oath the candidate also swears, that "a Master Mason's secrets, given to me in charge as such," * * "shall remain as secure and inviolate in my breast as in his own, murder and treason excepted, and they left to my own election." Now, this section of the oath is very broad, and may be understood to cover secrets of every description. But to put it beyond all doubt whether *crimes* are to be kept secret, murder and treason are excepted, showing that

the oath has respect particularly to concealing the crimes of a Master Mason. He may commit Theft, Robbery, Arson, Adultery, Rape, or any crime whatever, Murder and Treason excepted, and however well the commission of these crimes may be known to a Master Mason, if a Master Mason has committed them, he is under oath to conceal them. Now, is this right? Is this consistent with duty, either to God or man? Must not this often prove a fatal bar to the detection of crime, and the administration of justice? Certainly it must, or Freemasons must very frequently violate their solemn oath. If Freemasons deny this, in the denial they maintain that Masons care nothing for their oaths. It is self-evident that this Master's oath is either a conspiracy against the execution of law, or Master Masons care nothing for the solemnity of an oath. Gentlemen, take which horn of the dilemma you please! If these oaths are kept inviolate the course of justice must be effectually obstructed. If they are not kept, Master Masons are guilty of false swearing, and that continually. Which shall we believe to be true? Do Master Masons continually treat this solemn oath with contempt, or, do they respect their oaths, conceal the crimes of Master Masons, and fly to their rescue if they are detected and likely to be punished? Let not Master Masons, or any body else, exclaim: "Oh! these oaths are very innocent things! Crimes will be detected, criminals will be punished, for Masons care nothing for their oaths." Indeed! And does this excuse them? It is only by being guilty of false swearing that they can fail to thoroughly obstruct the course of justice. They are certainly under the most solemn oath to do that, in case of crime committed by a Master Mason, which will effectually defeat the execution of law. Let it be then particularly observed, that in every community where there are Master Masons, they either compose a class of conspirators against the administration of criminal law, and the execution of justice; or, they are a class of false swearers who care nothing for the solemnity of an oath. Let this not be regarded as a light thing. It is a most serious and important matter, and that which I have stated is neither false nor extravagant. It is a literal and solemn truth. Let it be well pondered. There is the oath; read it for yourself, mark its different points and promises, and you will see there is no escape from these conclusions.

5. The candidate in this oath swears, "I will not wrong this lodge, nor a brother of this degree to the value of one cent, knowingly my-

self, nor suffer it to be done by others, if in my power to prevent." Now observe, he makes this promise "under no less penalty, than to have my body severed in two in the midst, and divided to the north and south, my bowels burnt to ashes in the center, and scattered before the four winds of heaven, that there might not the least track or trace of remembrance remain among men or Masons of so vile or perjured a wretch as I should be, were I ever to prove willfully guilty of violating *any part* of this my solemn oath or obligation as Master Mason. So help me God, and keep me steadfast in the due performance of the same." Now, observe, one part of this Master's obligation is that which I have just quoted, that he will not wrong the lodge, nor a brother of this degree to the value of one cent. For doing this, he solemnly agrees to incur the awful penalty just above written. Is this just, as between man and man? Has any man a right to take such an oath under such penalties? Christian Freemason, can you see nothing wrong in this? Is not this profane, abominable, monstrous?

6. Observe, upon the same penalty, the candidate proceeds: "Furthermore do I promise and swear, that I will not be at the initiating, passing, and raising a candidate at one com

munication without a regular dispensation from the Grand Lodge for the same." Observe, then, to do this is so great a crime among Masons as to incur this awful penalty. The candidate proceeds: "Furthermore do I promise and swear, that I will not be at the initiating of an old man in his dotage, a young man in his nonage, an atheist, irreligious libertine, idiot, madman, hermaphrodite, nor woman." To do this, observe, is so great a crime among Masons as to incur the awful penalty attached to this oath. And this is Masonic benevolence! It professes to be a saving institution, and excludes the greater part of mankind from its benefits! The candidate proceeds: "Furthermore do I promise and swear, that I will not speak evil of a brother Master Mason, neither behind his back, nor before his face." Now, observe again, to do this is to incur this awful penalty, for this is *one part* of the oath. But who does not know that Freemasons violate this part of the oath, as well as that which relates to wronging each other, almost continually? The candidate proceeds: "Furthermore do I promise and swear, that I will not violate the chastity of a Master Mason's wife, sister, or daughter, I knowing them to be such, nor suffer it to be done by others, if in my power to prevent." But why not promise this in respect to all women? If this oath had included all **women**, it would have the appearance of justice and benevolence, but as it is, it is only an odious partiality, and does not imply even the semblance of virtue. The candidate proceeds: "Furthermore do I promise and swear, that I will support the constitution of the Grand Lodge of the State of ———, under which this lodge is held, and conform to all the by-laws, rules, and regulations of this or any other lodge of which I may, at any time hereafter, become a member." Observe that to violate this part of the obligation is to incur the awful penalty attached to this oath. The candidate proceeds: 'Furthermore do I promise and swear, that I will obey all regular signs, summonses, or tokens given, handed, sent, or thrown to me from the hand of a brother Master Mason, or from the body of a just and lawfully constituted lodge of such, provided it be within the length of my cable tow." This, indeed, puts a rope around the neck of every offending brother. He is under oath to answer any sign or summons given him from a brother Master Mason, or from a lodge. If he refuses or neglects to respond to the summons, he incurs the penalty, and is liable to have it executed upon him. The cable tow is literally a rope of several yards in length, but in a Master's Lodge is understood to represent three miles. In the degrees of Knighthood the distance is reckoned to be forty miles. This is fearful, and the responding to such summonses has, doubtless, cost many a man his life, by placing him in the hands of an exasperated lodge. The candidate proceeds: "Furthermore do I promise and swear, that I will go on a Master Mason's errand, whenever required, even should I have to go barefoot and bareheaded, if within the length of my cable tow." Now, failure to do this incurs the awful penalty of this obligation. A Master Mason's errand! What errand? From the words it would seem *any* errand, however trivial it may be; every errand, however frequently, a Master Mason might wish to send another on an errand. If it does not mean this, what does it mean? But whatever it means a failure incurs the whole penalty. The candidate proceeds: "Furthermore do I promise and swear, that I will always remember a brother Master Mason when on my knees offering up my devotions to Almighty God." But do Masons do this? In secret, family, public, social prayer, do they do this? Professed Christian Mason, do you do it? If not, you are guilty of false swearing every time you omit it. What! on your knees offering up your devotions to Almighty God, and guilty, at that very moment, of violating a solemn oath, by neglecting to pray for Master Masons! Remember, to fail in this respect incurs the awful penalty attached to this obligation. Now comes that part of the obligation upon which they lay so much stress as proving Masonry to be a benevolent institution: "Furthermore to I promise and swear, that I will be aiding and assisting all poor, indigent Master Masons, their wives and orphans, wherever disposed round the globe, as far as in my power, without injuring myself or family materially." In another place I shall show that there is no benevolence whatever in doing this, as every candidate pays into the public treasury money to compose a fund for the supply of the wants of the families of indigent Freemasons, simply upon the principle of a mutual insurance company. At present I simply remark that a failure to do this incurs the whole terrible penalty of this obligation. The candidate concludes his promises by saying: "Furthermore do I promise and swear, that if any part of this solemn oath and obligation be omitted at this time, I will hold myself amenable thereto, whenever informed."

Some months since I received a letter from a Master Mason who was manifestly a conscientious man. He informed me that he had been reading my letters in the *Independent*, on Freemasonry—that his mind was so distressed, in view of his Masonic obligations and relations, that he was wholly unable to attend to business, and that he should become deranged, if he could not escape from these entanglements—that he must and would renounce Freemasonry at all hazards. When he took the oath of the Master's degree the clause pledging him to keep a Master Mason's secrets, murder and treason excepted, was omitted, so that he was not aware of that clause until afterward. This clause, however, that I last quoted, bound him fast. No wonder that this conscientious man was frightened when he came to understand his true position. In administering this long oath to any conscientious man, any part of it that would shock a tender conscience may be omitted, and yet the candidate is pledged to hold himself amenable to that part, or those parts, that have been omitted, whenever informed of the same. This is a trap and a snare into which many a tender conscience has been betrayed. And is this an oath which a Christian man may take, or any other man, without sin? Can any man administer this oath, or take it, or be voluntarily present, aiding and abetting, and be guiltless of awful profanity and blasphemy? I have dwelt the longer upon this oath, because probably two-thirds of the Masons in the United States have gone no further than this degree. Now, is it not perfectly plain that a man who has taken this oath ought not to be intrusted with the office of a magistrate, a sheriff, marshal or constable? That he is not to be credited as a witness where a Master Mason is a party? That he ought not to be allowed a place on a jury where a Master Mason is a party? And, in short, that he can not safely be intrusted with any office of honor or profit, either in Church or State? Is it not plain that a Master's Lodge, in any community, is a dangerous institution, and that the whole country is interested in the utter suppression of such an institution?

Let not this opinion be regarded as too severe. The fact is that Freemasons intend to fulfill their vows, or they do not. If Master Masons intend to do what they swear to do, is it right to intrust them with the execution of the laws? If they do *not* intend to fulfill their vows, of what avail will their oath of office be, since they have no regard for the solemnity of an oath? In every view of the subject it is plain that such men ought not to be trusted. Take either horn of the dilemma, it amounts to the same thing. I shall have more to say on this subject hereafter.

## CHAPTER VII.

## ROYAL ARCH DEGREE.

THE fourth degree of Masonry is that of "Mark Master." The fifth is that of "Past Master." The sixth is that of "Most Excellent Master." In these the same points, in substance, are sworn to as in the Master's degree. In each succeeding oath the candidate recognizes and reaffirms all of his past obligations. In nearly every obligation the candidates swear implicit allegiance to the Grand Lodge of the United States and to the Grand Lodge of the State under which his lodge holds its charter. The candidate swears, also, that he will never be present at the raising of any person to a higher degree who has not regularly taken each and all of the previous or lower degrees. In the first degree secresy alone is enjoined. After this, additional clauses are introduced at every step, until the oaths of some of the higher degrees spread over several pages. They nearly all pledge pecuniary help to poor, indigent, worthy Masons, and their families, as far as they can *without material injury to themselves and families*. They never promise to *deny themselves* or *families* any comfort or luxury for the purpose of helping indigent, worthy Masons or their families. They never promise in their oaths to give pecuniary aid to any but Masons and their families. These families, by their head, have paid into the Masonic fund the amount that entitles them to aid, in case of pecuniary want, on the principle of mutual insurance against want.

All Masons above the third, or Master's degree, are sworn to keep inviolate the secrets of a brother, murder and treason excepted, up to the seventh, or Royal Arch degree. In the oath of this degree the candidate, as we shall see, swears to keep all the secrets of a companion of this degree, *murder and treason not excepted*. All Masons *of* and *above* this degree are solemnly bound to do this. The same is true of all the points sworn to in this obligation which we proceed to examine.

In reviewing this and the degrees above it, I shall not need to give them in full, as they are substantially and almost verbatim alike, except as new points are added as the candidate goes on from one degree to another. The Royal

Arch degree is taken in a lodge called a chapter. A Mason of this degree is called a companion, while in the lower degrees Masons address each other as brothers. After swearing to the same points contained in previously taken oaths, the kneeling candidate, with hands on the Holy Bible, proceeds: "I furthermore promise and swear, that I will aid and assist a companion Royal Arch Mason when engaged in any difficulty, and espouse his cause so far as to extricate him from the same, if within my power, *whether he be right or wrong.*

Here, then, we have a class of men sworn, under most frightful penalties, to espouse the cause of a companion so far as to extricate him from any difficulty, to the extent of their power, whether he is *right* or *wrong.* How can such a man be safely intrusted with any office connected with the administration of the law? He means to abide by and perform this solemn oath, or he does not. If he does, will he not inevitably defeat the due execution of law, if intrusted with office connected with it? Suppose he is a magistrate, a sheriff, marshal, or constable, will he not be able to prevent the execution of justice, if he does all within his power, as he is solemnly sworn to do? If on a jury, if sworn as a witness, how can he be trusted, if he fulfills his Masonic vows?

But suppose he does not intend to abide by and fulfill his vows, but still adheres, and does not renounce them; suppose he still recognizes their obligation, but fails to fulfill them, is he a man to be trusted with an office? If he does not respect and fulfill his Masonic oaths, the validity of which he acknowledges by continued adherence, of what avail will be his oath of office? Of what use will it be for him to swear that he will faithfully execute the laws, if he has taken the oath of this degree, and either fulfills or fails to fulfill it? If he fulfills it, he surely will not execute the law upon a companion Royal Arch Mason. If he still adheres to, but fails to fulfill his oath, he does not respect the solemnity of an oath, and ought not to be intrusted with an office. If he publicly, sincerely, and penitently renounces his Masonic oath as unlawful, profane, and not binding, he may be trusted with office, but while he adheres he must violate either his oath of office, or his Masonic oath, whenever the accused is a Royal Arch Mason, and, indeed, whenever such an one is involved in any legal difficulty.

I beseech the public not to think this *severe*. There is, in fact, no third way. Take either horn of the dilemma and it amounts to the same thing. To treat this lightly, as some are disposed to do, or to get over it under cover of the plea of charity, is worse than nonsense; it is wicked to ignore the truth, and proceed as if there were no great wrong in this case. There is great wrong, great sin, and great danger in this case—danger to both *Church* and *State*, danger to the *souls* of men thus situated. I beseech this class of men to consider this matter, and renounce this position. If they will not, I see neither justice nor safety in allowing such men to hold an office in Church or State.

But what is the moral character of a man who espouses the cause, and does all he can to rescue a criminal from the hands of justice? I answer, he is a partaker of his guilt. He is truly an accessory after the fact. This oath does not contemplate the professsional services of an advocate employed to defend an accused person in a court of justice. But even in this case an advocate has no right to defeat the due administration of justice, and turn the criminal loose to prey upon society. When he does this he sins both against God and society. It is his business to see that no injustice is done the accused; to secure for him a fair and impartial trial, but not to rescue him, if guilty. An advocate who would "espouse the cause" of a criminal "so far as to extricate him from his difficulty, whether right or wrong," would deserve the execration of both God and man.

The candidate in this degree proceeds, as follows: "Also, that I will promote a companion Royal Arch Mason's political preferment in preference to another of equal qualifications." Bernard, who has taken this and many other Masonic oaths, says, in his "Light on Masonry," in a foot-note, that this clause of the oath is, in some chapters, made a distinct point in the obligation, thus: "I furthermore promise and swear, that I will vote for a companion Royal Arch Mason before any other of equal qualifications," and in some chapters both are left out of the obligation. Upon this clause I remark:

1. Freemasons deny that Freemasonry has anything to do with any man's political opinions, or actions, provided he be not the enemy of his country. From this obligation, or oath he can judge of the truth or falsehood of this profession. Again, who does not know that thousands of the Southern rebels were and are accepted Freemasons. How does this fact comport with the pretense that a Freemason must be loyal to the government under which he lives. In the higher degrees they swear to

be loyal and true to their government, but are the Southern Masons so?

---

2. We see why such efforts are made to increase the number of Royal Arch Masons, and the reasons held out to induce political aspirants to become Royal Arch Masons. It is said, I suppose truly, that Royal Arch Masons are multiplying by scores of thousands in this country. It is, beyond doubt, the design of their leaders to control the elections and secure the offices throughout the country. From letters received from reliable parties I learn that in some localities Masons avow this design. But whether they avow or deny it, this oath unmistakably reveals their design. Why is this clause found in this oath? It is presumption and foolhardiness to ignore this plain revelation of their design to control the government, secure the offices, and have everything their own way. If the public can not be aroused to look this conspiracy in the face, and rise up and put it down in time, they will surely find, too late, that their hands are tied, and that virtual slavery or a bloody revolution awaits us. Our children and grandchildren will reap the bitter fruits of our own folly and credulity. What do Freemasons mean by this oath? They either intend to keep it, or *not* to keep it. If

they mean to do as they have promised under the most solemn oath to do, then Freemasonry, at least Freemasonry of this and all the higher degrees, is a political conspiracy to secure the offices and the control of the government. I say Freemasonry of this and of *all the higher degrees*, for be it remembered that all Masons of and above this degree have taken the oath of this degree. I quote the following from an able editorial in the *Albany Evening Journal Extra*, October 27, 1831: "An addition was made to the *Master's* oath, in the northern part of this State, a few years since, by Gov. Pitcher, who introduced it from Vermont. It was to the effect that, in voting for officers, a preference should be given to a Mason over another candidate of equal qualifications. Very respectable testimony of the fact was published very generally in the newspapers, about two years since, and has never, to the knowledge of the writer, been contradicted or questioned. It is admitted that this obligation, in terms, has not generally been administered (that is, in a Master's Lodge), but it is insisted that if the principle be once admitted that men in our country may band together in secret conclave, for any purpose not known to the laws, and may bind themselves under obligations involving the penalty of *death* for their transgressions, they may as well pledge themselves to any new object, or purpose, as to those for which they have already associated There is no limit to the extent of such associations, if they are allowed at all. The principle itself is radically wrong. But independent of any positive obligation, the very creation of such artificial ties of brotherhood, the strength which they acquire by frequent repetition and by the associations of the fraternity, necessarily produce a clannish attachment which will ordinarily exhibit itself in the most important concerns of life in bestowing business and patronage on a brother, and in elevating him to office and rank which will reflect back honor upon the order to which he belongs. The inevitable result, therefore, of such institutions is to give one class of citizens unequal and unjust advantages over those who are not of the favored order. And when we find this natural result hastened and strengthened by obligations, under the most awful penalties, to fly to the relief of a brother, to espouse his cause, whether right or wrong, and to conceal his crimes, have not the rest of the community a right to say to these exclusives, these privileged orders, "we will not submit to your usurpations, and until you restore your fellow-citizens to equal rights and privileges with you, we will not give you our votes or trust you with public office." To these remarks I fully subscribe. But I return to another clause of this oath. The candidate proceeds: "Furthermore do I promise and swear, that a companion Royal Arch Mason's secrets, given me in charge as such, and I knowing them to be such, shall remain as secure and inviolable in my breast as in his own, *murder and treason not excepted.*" Bernard says, in a foot-note, "In some chapters this is administered, 'All the secrets of a companion, without exception.'" Upon this clause I remark:

1. That Freemasonry waxes worse and worse as you ascend from the lower to the higher degrees. It will be remembered that in the Master's oath murder and treason were excepted in the oath of secrecy. In this degree murder and treason are *not* excepted. Now, as all Masons who take the degrees above this have also taken this oath, it follows that all that army of Freemasons, composed of Royal Arch Masons, and all who have taken the degrees above this, are under the most solemn oath to conceal each other's crimes, without exception. And what an institution is this, to to be allowed existence under any government, *especially* under a republican form of government! Is it safe to have such a set of

men scattered broadcast over all the United States? Let us look this thing squarely in the face. It can not be honestly denied that Royal Arch Masons take this oath. But a short time since a minister of the Gospel of my acquaintance was confronted with this oath, and he did not deny having taken it. Now, if all that vast army of Masons who have taken this oath intend to do as they swear to do, what must be the result? Scores and hundreds of thousands of men, scattered broadcast over the whole land, are pledged by the most solemn oath, and under the penalty of death, to conceal each other's crimes, without exception. Are such men to be safely intrusted with office, either in Church or State? And must not a government be on the verge of ruin when such a conspiracy is allowed to multiply its numbers at such a frightful rate as it is doing, at this time, in this country? Will the people of the United States have the foolhardiness to ignore the crime and danger of this conspiracy against their liberty? Or will they good-naturedly assume that Freemasons *mean* no such thing? Why, then, is this oath? Will they, under the cover of mock charity, assume that these men *will* not cover up each other's crimes? What kind of charity is this? Is it **charity** to believe that a set of men will *lie* under oath, as all Freemasons above the degree of Fellow Craft *must* do, if they do not conceal each other's crimes? Again, what right have Freemasons, themselves, to complain of a want of charity in those who regard them as conspirators against good government? Why, what shall we do? If they do not repent of, and renounce, these oaths, we *must* either regard them as conspirators against government, or as men who will *lie*, under the solemnity of a most awful oath. The gentlemen must choose which horn of the dilemma they will take. On the one hand, they are sworn conspirators against the execution of the criminal laws; on the other, they are a class of men that do not regard the solemnity of an oath. This is the exact truth, and it is folly and madness to ignore it. Freemasons, therefore, have no right to complain of us, if we take them at their word, and believe that they *mean* to do what they have *sworn* they will do. They demand charity of us. Is it not charitable to believe that they intend to fulfill such solemn vows, made, and often repeated, under such terrible sanctions? The candidate of this degree concludes by saying: "Binding myself under no less penalty than that of having my skull smote off, and my brains exposed to the scorching rays of the sun, should I ever, knowingly or willfully, violate or transgress *any part* of this, my solemn oath or obligation as a Royal Arch Mason. So help me, God, and keep me steadfast in the performance of the same." Now, upon this awful sanction, the candidate swears that he will not wrong the chapter, or a companion of this degree, out of anything, or suffer it to be done by others, if in his power to prevent it. Men in certain business partnerships and relations, whose partners have been Royal Arch Masons, have been influenced to take this degree to prevent their being wronged by their Masonic partners. On the best authority, I have been informed of one case of this kind, recently, and it turned out that while the one who was thus induced to take this degree was in the army, fighting the battles of his country, his Royal Arch partner deliberately cheated him out of several thousand dollars. What shall we say to, what shall we do with, these men who swarm in every part of this country, and who are thus banded together to espouse each other's cause and to extricate each other from any difficulty, whether they are right or wrong, to conceal each other's crimes, to vote each other into office, and the like? Can wholesome society continue to exist under the influence of such an institution as this?

## CHAPTER VIII.

## SWORN TO PERSECUTE.

MASONS *are sworn to persecute unto death anyone who violates Masonic obligation.* In the oath of the THRICE ILLUSTRIOUS ORDER of the CROSS the candidate swears, as follows, "Light on Masonry," eighth edition, page 199: "You further swear, that should you know another to violate any essential point of this obligation, you will use your most decided endeavors, *by the blessing of God*, to bring such person to the *strictest and most condign punishment, agreeably to the rules and usages of our ancient fraternity;* and this, by pointing him out to the world as an unworthy vagabond, by opposing his interest, by deranging his business, by transferring his character after him wherever he may go, and by exposing him to the contempt of the whole fraternity and of the world, during his whole natural life." The penalty of this obligation is as follows: "To all and every part thereof we then bind you, and by ancient usage you bind yourself, under the no less infamous penalty than dying the death of a traitor, by having a spear, or other sharp instrument, like our Divine Master, thrust into your left side, bearing testimony, even in death, to the power and justice of the mark of the Holy Cross." Upon this obligation I remark:

1. Here we have an explanation of the notorious fact that Freemasons try, in every way, to ruin the reputation of all who renounce Masonry. The air has almost been darkened by the immense number of falsehoods that have been circulated, by Freemasons, to destroy the reputation of every man who has renounced Freemasonry, and published it to the world, or has written against it. No pains have been spared to destroy all confidence in the testimony of such men. Does not this oath render it impossible for us to believe what Freemasons say of the character of those who violate their obligations? Who of us that lived forty years ago does not remember how Freemasons endeavored to destroy the reputation of William Morgan, of Elder Bernard, of Elder Stearns, and also of Mr. Allyn, and who that is at all acquainted with facts does not know that the utmost pains are taken to destroy the reputation

of every man that dares to take his pen and expose their institution. When I had occasion to quote Elder Bernard's book, in preaching on the subject of Freemasonry a few months ago, I was told in the streets, before I got home, that he was a man of bad character. I knew better, and knew well how to understand such representations, for this is the way in which the testimony of all such men is sought to be disposed of by Freemasons. Will this be denied? What, then, is the meaning of this oath? Are not Masons under oath to do this? Indeed they are. A few months since I received the following letter. For reasons which will be appreciated, I omit name and date. The writer says: "About a week since, a man calling himself *Professor W. E. Moore, the great South American explorer*, came to this place, lecturing on Freemasonry. He is a Mason, and has given private lectures to the lodges here, and has lectured once before the public. He claims to have been at Oberlin, recently, and that while there he had an interview with you, and that he tested you sufficiently to satisfy himself that you had never been a Mason; and further, he says that the conversation he had with you resulted to his great satisfaction, and to your great discomfiture." At nearly the same date of this letter, I received, from the same place, a letter from a Freemason of my acquaintance, giving substantially the same account of this Professor Moore. In this letter, however, it is added that his conversation with me compelled me to confess that I never had been a Mason, and to say I would publish no more against Masonry. This last letter I have mislaid, so that I can not lay my hand upon it. From the first I quote *verbatim et literatim*. I replied to these letters, as I now assert, that every word of what this man says of me is false. That I never saw or heard of this man, to my knowledge, until I received those letters. But this is nothing new or strange. Such false representations are just what we are to expect, if Freemasons of this and the higher degrees fulfill their vows. Why should they be believed, and how can they complain of us for not believing what they say of men who have renounced Masonry and oppose it? It is mere folly and madness to believe them. It is not difficult, if Freemasons desire it, to produce almost any amount of testimony to prove that every manner and degree of falsehood is resorted to to destroy the testimony of men who witness against them. Any man who will renounce these horrid oaths, and expose their profanity to the public, should make up his mind beforehand to endure any amount of slander and persecution which the **ingenuity** of Freemasons can invent.

In the degree of Knights Adepts of the Eagle or Sun, "Light on Masonry," eighth edition, page 269, we have the following: "*The man peeping.* By the man you saw peeping, and who was discovered, and seized, and conducted to death, *is an emblem of those who come to be initiated into our sacred mysteries through a motive of curiosity; and if so indiscreet as to divulge their obligations*, WE ARE BOUND TO CAUSE THEIR DEATH, AND TAKE VENGEANCE ON THE TREASON BY THE DESTRUCTION OF THE TRAITORS!!!" Here we find that Freemasons of this and the higher degrees are solemnly pledged to destroy the lives of those who violate their obligations. Deacon William A. Bartlett, of Pella, Iowa, in his public renunciation of Freemasonry, says—"Letters on Masonry," by Elder John G. Stearns, page 169—" During the winter or spring following my initiation, a resolution was offered in the lodge for adoption, and to be published outside the lodge, condemning the abduction of Morgan. After much discussion, the Worshipful Master called another to the chair, and said, 'Brethren, what do you mean by offering such a resolution as this? Had we been at Batavia, we would have done just what those brethren have done, and *taken the life of Morgan*, because the oaths of Masonry demand it at our hands. And will you condemn brethren for doing what you would have done had you been there? I trust not.' When the vote to condemn them was taken, but *three* voted in favor of the resolution." There is abundant proof that Freemasons generally, at first, denied the murder of Morgan, and when they could no longer have courage to deny it, they *justified* it, until public indignation was so much aroused as to make them ashamed to justify it. Let those who wish for proof on the question of their justifying it read the volume of Elder Stearns, to be had at the bookstores, and he will find evidence enough of the fact.

## CHAPTER IX.

## AWFUL PROFANITY OF MASONIC OATHS.

IN the degree of Templar and Knight of Malta, as found in the *seventh* edition of "Light on Masonry," page 182, in a lecture in which the candidate is giving an account of what he had passed through, he says: "I then took the cup (the upper part of the human skull) in my hand, and repeated, after the Grand Commander, the following obligation: 'This pure wine I now take in testimony of my belief in the mortality of the body and the immortality of the soul—and may this libation appear as a witness against me both here and hereafter—and as the sins of the world were laid upon the head of the Savior, so may all the sins committed by the person whose skull this was be heaped upon my head, in addition to my own, should I ever; knowingly or willfully, violate or transgress any obligation that I have heretofore taken, take at this time, or shall at any future period take, in relation to any degree of Masonry or order of Knighthood. So help me God?" Now, observe what a horrid imprecation is here. These Knights Templar and Knights of Malta take their oaths sustained by such a horrid penalty as this. They say that they will incur this penalty, not merely if they violate the peculiar obligation of this degree, but "any obligation that I have heretofore taken, take at this time, or shall at any future period take, in relation to any degree of Masonry or order of Knighthood." This is called "the sealed obligation." Here, in the most solemn manner, the candidate, drinking wine out of a human skull, takes upon himself this obligation, under the penalty of a double damnation. What can exceed the profanity and wickedness of this?

On the 185th page of the same book, we find a note quoted from the work of Brother Allyn, who renounced Masonry and published on the subject. I will quote the note entire. Mr. Allyn says of the fifth libation, or *sealed obligation*, it "is referred to by Templars in confidential communications, relative to matters of great importance, when other Masonic obligations seem insufficient to secure *secresy, silence, and safety.* Such, for instance, was the murder of William Morgan, which was communicated from one Templar to another, under the pledge, and upon this sealed obligation." He also remarks, in another place: "When I received this degree I objected to drink from the human skull, and to take the *profane oath* required by the rules of the order. I observed to the Most Eminent that I supposed that that part of the ceremonies would be dispensed with. The Sir Knights charged upon me, and the Most Eminent said: 'Pilgrim, you here see the swords of your companions drawn to defend you in the discharge of every *duty we* require of you. They are also drawn *to avenge any violation of the rules of our order.* We expect you to proceed.' A clergyman, an acquaintance of mine, came forward, and said: 'Companion Allyn, this part of the ceremonies is never dispensed with. I, and all the Sir Knights, have drank from the cup and taken the fifth libation. It is perfectly proper, and will be qualified to your satisfaction.' I then drank of the cup of double damnation."

Now, can any profanity be more horrible than this? And yet there is nothing in Masonry, we are told, that is at all inconsistent with the Christian religion! On the 187th page of the same volume, the "Knight of the Christian Mark," at the conclusion of his obligation, says: "All this I promise in the name of the Father, of the Son, and of the Holy Ghost; and if I perform it not, let me be ANATHEMA MARANATHA! ANATHEMA MARANATHA!!" Anathema Maranatha is understood to mean accursed at the Lord's coming. Again, the "Knights of the Red Cross" take their obligations upon the following penalty, page 164: "To all of which I do most solemnly promise and swear, binding myself under no less penalty than that of having my house torn down, the timbers thereof set up, and I hanged thereon; and when the last trump shall blow, that I be forever excluded from the society of all true and courteous Knights, should I ever, willfully or knowingly, violate any part of this solemn obligation of Knight of the Red Cross. So help me, God, and keep me steadfast to keep and perform the same."

The "Knights of the Eagle, and Sovereign Prince of Rose Croix de Heroden," in receiving this degree, pass through the following, page 253, of Bernard's eighth edition of "Light on Masonry:" "During this time the brethren in the second department take off their black decorations, and put on the red, and, also, uncover the jewels. The candidate knocks on the door, and the Warden, for answer, shuts the door in his face. The **Master** of Ceremonies says: 'These marks of indignity are not sufficiently humiliating; you must pass through more rigorous proofs, before you can find it.' He then takes off the candidate the chasuble and black apron, and puts over him a black cloth, covered with ashes and dust, and says to him: 'I am going to conduct you into the darkest and most dismal place, from whence the word shall triumphantly come to the glory and advantage of Masonry.' He then takes him into the third apartment, and takes from him his covering, and makes him go three times around (showing him the representation of the torments of the damned), when he is led to the door of the chapter, and the Master of Ceremonies says to him: '*The horrors which yon have just now seen are but a faint representation of those you shall suffer, if you break through our laws, or infringe the obligation you have taken.*'" In a footnote, the editor says: " This certainly caps the climax, and renders the institution of Masonry complete. The torments of the damned, the awful punishment which the Almighty inflicts on the violators of his righteous law is but a *faint emblem* of the punishment which Masonry here declares *shall be inflicted on the violators of Masonic law*, or those who are guilty of an infraction of Masonic obligations!" But I get sick of pursuing these loathsome and blasphemous details; and I fear I shall so shock my readers that they will be as wearied as I am myself. In reading over these oaths, it would seem as if a Masonic lodge was a place where men had assembled to commit the utmost blasphemy of which they were capable, to mock and scoff at all that is sacred, and to beget among themselves the utmost contempt for every form of moral obligation. These oaths sound as if the men who were taking and administering them were determined to annihilate their moral sense, and to render themselves incapable of making any moral discriminations, and certainly, if they can see no sin in taking and administering such oaths under such penalties, they have succeeded, whether intentionally or not, in rendering themselves utterly blind, as regards the moral character of their conduct. By repeating their blasphemy they have put out their own eyes. Now these oaths mean something, or they do not. Masons, when they take them, mean to abide by them, or they do not. If they do not, to take them is blasphemy. If they do mean to abide by them, they are sworn to perform deeds, not only the most injurious to society, to government, and the church of God of any that can well be named, but they swear, in case of the violation of any point of these obligations, to seek to have the penalties inflicted on the violator. In other words, in such a case, they swear to commit murder; and every man who adheres to such obligations is under oath to seek to accomplish the violent death, not only of every man who shall betray the secrets, but, also, of everyone who shall violate *any point* or *part* of these obligations. Now, the solemn question arises, are these oaths a mere farce, a mere taking of the name of God in vain, in the most trifling manner, and under the most solemn circumstances? or, are we to understand that the Masonic institution is a *conspiracy*, its members taking, in all seriousness and good faith, such horrid oaths to do such horrid deeds, upon such horrid penalties? Which are we to understand to be true? If *either* is true, I ask the church of God, I ask the world, what more abominable institution ever existed than this? And yet we are told that in all this trifling with oaths, or, if not trifling, this horrid conspiracy, there is nothing inconsistent with the Christian religion! And even ministers of the Gospel are found who can justify it and eulogize it in a manner most profane, and even blasphemous.

Now, in charity, I suppose it to be **true that** the great mass of Masons, who are nominally so, and who have, in a hurry and under great excitement, taken more or less of the degrees, have only a very confused conception of what Masonry really is. Surely, if Masons really understood what Masonry is, as it is delineated in these books, no Christian Mason would think himself at liberty to remain another day a member of the fraternity. The fact is, a great many *nominal* Masons are not so in *reality.* It is as plain as possible that a man, *knowing what it is, and embracing it in his heart, can not be a Christian man.* To say he can is to belie the very nature of Christianity.

But here let me ask, in concluding this article, *what is there in Masonry to justify the taking of such oaths, under such penalties?* If there is any *good* in Masonry, why should it be concealed? and why should such oaths be taken to conceal it? If Masonry is an *evil* thing, and its secrets are evil, of course, to take any oath to conceal the wickedness is utterly unjustifiable. Does Masonry exact these oaths for the sake of concealing from outsiders the miserable falsehoods that they palm off upon their candidates, which everywhere abound in Masonry? But what is there in these stories, if true, that should be concealed? If Hiram Abiff was murdered. as Masons pretend; if the Ark of the Covenant, with its sacred contents, was really found in the vault under ground, as Masons pretend, is there any justifiable reason for concealing from the whole world these facts I have sought in vain for a reason to justify the taking of any oaths at all in Masonry And it is passing strange that such oaths under such penalties, should ever have been so much as dreamed of by Masons as being justified by their secrets. The fact is, their stringent secrecy must be designed, in part, to excite the curiosity of men, and draw candidates into the snare. The highest Masonic authority has affirmed that *their secrecy is essential to their existence;* and that, if their secrets were exposed, the institution could not live. Now, this is no doubt true, and is the great reason, as I conceive, for guarding their secrets with such horrid oaths. But I said, in an early number, that Masonry is a *swindle.* Where are the important secrets which they promise to their candidates? For what do the candidates pay their money but really to be imposed upon? But it may be well asked, why do Masons, once embarked in Masonry, go on, from one degree to another multiplying their oaths, obligations, and imprecations? When they are once within a lodge to take a degree, they dare not do otherwise than to go forward. I could quote numerous instances from the writings of seceding Masons showing how they have been urged from step to step, and assured, if they would proceed, that everything would be explained to their satisfaction. They have been told, as in the case of Mr. Allyn just noticed, that everything would be qualified and explained to their satisfaction. Upon Mr. Allyn, as we have seen, the Sir Knights *drew their swords* when he hesitated to go forward; and the Most Eminent informed him that he must go forward, or their swords would avenge his disobedience.

The fact is, when once within the lodge, they dare not stop short of taking the obligation belonging to the degree; and they are persuaded by those who have taken higher degrees, to go forward from one degree to another.

And the great Masonic argument to keep them steadfast in concealing the imposition that has been practiced upon them, and to persuade them not to renounce and expose what they have passed through, is, that of having their throats cut, their tongues torn out by the roots, their heart and vitals torn out and thrown to the vultures of the air, drowning and murder.

Masons profess not to invite or persuade any to join the lodges; and the candidates, when they come forward for their degrees, are asked if they come forward of their own free will and accord. To this, of course, they answer, yes.

But what has made them willing? *They have been persuaded to it.* They have been invited to join;—they have been *urged* to join; motives of self-interest have been set before them in such a light as to gain their consent They are thus made willing; and, therefore, truthfully say, that they do it of their own free will and accord.

But it is almost, if not quite, the universal testimony of renouncing Masons, that they were persuaded to it. They were made willing to join by such representations as overpersuaded them. I do not believe that one in five hundred of those who join the Masonic lodge, join without being persuaded to do so. But let me say also, that the great mass of Freemasons have never taken more than the first three degrees. They may know nothing about the higher degrees. *Now in what sense are they responsible for the wickedness of the institution as revealed in the higher degrees?* I answer, they would not be responsible at all, if they neither knew anything of those degrees, nor had any *opportunity* to know anything of them.

But as these books have been widely circulated, and are secretly kept by Masons, and are better known to Freemasons at present by far than they are to the outward world,—those who have taken the lower degrees, if they continue to sustain the institution, which is in reality a unit, become morally responsible for the wickedness of the higher degrees. But the obligations in the first three degrees are by no means innocent. They are such obligations as no man has any right to take or to administer. To adhere to the institution is to indorse it. But again, why do not Freemasons now, who have these books, and who know, or *ought* to know thoroughly the nature, designs, and tendency of the institution, publicly renounce the whole thing, confess their sin, and proclaim their independence of the order? I answer, first—They have seared their consciences by what they have done, and have, therefore, very little sense of the great sinfulness of remaining a member of such an abominable institution. I must say that I am utterly amazed at the want of conscientiousness among Masons on this subject. As I have said, they have put out the eyes of their moral sense, and do not at all appreciate the awful guilt of their position. And, secondly— They *dare* not. And if by their oaths they *mean* anything, it is not to be wondered at that they are *afraid* to renounce Freemasonry. Why the fraternity are under oath to persecute them, to represent them as perjured vagabonds, to destroy their characters, their business, and their influence, and to follow them from place to place, transferring their character after them during their whole natural life. This surely is enough to deter common men from renouncing their allegiance to the institution. To be sure, this danger does not excuse them; but weak as human nature is, it is not wonderful that it has its influence.

But again, Masons are under oath, if they renounce the order, to seek the destruction of *their lives*. And they have given terrible proof that their oaths are not a dead letter in this respect, not only in the murder of William Morgan, but of many others who have renounced their allegiance to the brotherhood. In a sermon which lies before me, delivered by Rev Moses Thacher, a man well known in the Christian world, and who has himself taken many degrees of Masonry, he says:

"The institution is dangerous to civil and religious rights. It is stained with *blood*. I have *reliable historical evidence of not less than seven individuals, including Morgan, murdered under Masonic law.*" Since this sermon was preached other cases have come to light, and are constantly coming to light, in which persons have been murdered for disclosing Masonic secrets. And if the truth shall ever be known in this world, I believe it will be found that scores of persons, in this and other countries, have been murdered for unfaithfulness to Masonic obligations. Freemasons understand quite well the malignity of the spirit of Freemasonry. They understand that it will not argue, that it will not discuss the reasonableness or unreasonableness, the virtue or the sin of the institution; but that its argument is *assassination*. I am now daily in the receipt of letters from various parts of the country, expressing the highest satisfaction that anybody can be found who dares write against the institution at this day. The fact is, there are a great many men belonging to the institution, who are heartily sick of it, and would fain be rid of it; but who dare not open their mouths or whisper to any individual in the world their secret abhorrence of the institution. But it is time *to speak out*. And

I do beg my brethren in the ministry, and the whole Christian Church, to examine it for themselves, and not turn away from looking the evil in the face until it is too late.

## CHAPTER X.

## PERVERSE AND PROFANE USE OF THE HOLY BIBLE.

IN this number I wish to call the attention of my readers to some of the cases in which Freemasons misapply and misrepresent, and most profanely, if not blasphemously, use the Holy Scriptures. I will not go far into the sickening details; but far enough, I trust, to lead serious persons to reflect upon the nature of a society that can trifle with such solemn things.

The "Knights of the East and West" take the following oath, and then pass through the following ceremonies:—See pp. 214—220 of the first edition, or eighth edition, 230—240, of Bernard's Light on Masonry—"I———, do promise and solemnly swear and declare, in the awful presence of the only One Most Holy Puissant, Almighty, and Most Merciful Grand Architect of Heaven and Earth, who created the universe and myself through His infinite goodness, and conducts it with wisdom and justice, and in the presence of the Most Excellent and Upright Princes and Knights of the East and West, here present in convocation and grand council, on my sacred word of honor, and under every tie both moral and religious, that I never will reveal to any person whomsoever below me, or to whom the same may not belong by being legally and lawfully initiated, the secrets of this degree which are now about to be communicated to me, under the penalty of not only being dishonored, but *to consider my life as the immediate forfeiture*, and that *to be taken from me with all the tortures and pains* to be inflicted *in manner as I have consented to in my preceding degrees.* I further solemnly promise and swear that I will *pay due obedience and submission to all the degrees beyond this*, &c. All this I solemnly swear and sincerely promise upon my sacred word of honor, under the penalty of the severe wrath of the Almighty Creator of Heaven and Earth; and may He have mercy on my soul in the great and awful day of judgment agreeably to my conformity thereto. Amen. Amen. Amen. The All Puissant then takes the ewer filled with perfumed ointment, and anoints his head, eyes, mouth, heart, the tip of his right ear, nand, and foot. and says, "You are now, my dear brother, received a member of our society. You will recollect to live up to the precepts of it; and also, *remember that those parts of your body which have the greatest power of assisting you in good or evil, have this day been made holy.*" The Master of Ceremonies then places the candidate between the two Wardens, with the draft before him. The Senior Warden says to him, "Examine with deliberation and attention everything which the All Puissant is going to show you." After a short pause, he, the S. W., says, "Is there mortal here worthy to open the book with the seven seals?" All the brethren cast their eyes down and sigh. The Senior Warden hearing their sighs, says to them, "Venerable and respectable brethren, be not afflicted here is a victim (pointing to the candidate) whose courage will give you content."

S. W. to the candidate, " Do you know the reason why the ancients have a long beard?"

CAN. "I do not, but I presume you do."

S. W. "They are those who came here after passing through great tribulation, and having washed their robes in their own blood: will you purchase your robes at so great a price?"

CAN. "Yes; I am willing."

The Wardens then conduct him to the basin, and bare both his arms; they place a ligature on each, the same as in performing the operation of blood-letting. Each Warden being armed with a lancet, makes an incision in each of his arms just deep enough to draw a drop of blood, which is wiped on a napkin, and then shown to the brethren. The Senior Warden then says, "See, my brethren, a man who has spilled his blood to acquire a knowledge of your mysteries, and shrunk not from the trial."

Then the All Puissant opens the FIRST SEAL of the great book, and takes from thence a *bone quiver* filled with arrows, and a crown, and gives them to one of the Ancients, and says to him, "Depart and continue the conquest." He opens the SECOND SEAL, and takes out a *sword*, and gives it to the next aged, and says, "Go and destroy peace among the profane and wicked brethren, that they may never appear in our Council." He opens the THIRD SEAL, and takes a *balance*, and gives it to the next aged, and says, "Dispense rigid justice to the profane and wicked brethren." He opens the FOURTH SEAL, and takes out a *skull*, and gives it to the next aged, and says, "Go and endeavor to convince the wicked that death is the reward of their guilt." He opens the FIFTH SEAL, and takes out a *cloth* stained with blood, and gives it to the next aged, and says,

"When is the time (or the time will arrive) that *we shall revenge* and *punish* the profane and wicked, who have destroyed so many of their brethren by false accusations." He opens the SIXTH SEAL, and that moment the sun is darkened and the moon stained with blood! He opens the SEVENTH SEAL, and takes out *incense*, which he gives to a brother, and also a *vase*, with *seven trumpets*, and gives one to each of the seven aged brethren. After this the four *old man* in the four corners show their inflated bladders (beeves bladders filled with wind, under their arms), representing the four winds, when the All Puissant says: "Here is seen the fulfillment of a prophecy (Rev. vii. 3); strike not nor punish the profane and wicked of our order until I have selected the true and worthy Masons." Then the four winds raise their bladders, and one of the trumpets sounds, when the two Wardens cover the candidate's arms, and take from him his apron and jewels of the last degree. The second trumpet sounds, when the Junior Warden gives the candidate the apron and jewel of this degree. The third trumpet sounds, when the Senior Warden gives him a long beard. The fourth trumpet sounds, and the Junior Warden gives him a crown of gold. The fifth trumpet sounds, and the Senior Warden gives him a girdle of gold. The sixth trumpet sounds, and the Junior Warden gives him the sign, token, and words. The seventh trumpet sounds, on which they all sound together, when the Senior Warden conducts the candidate to the vacant canopy.

[This canopy, it will be recollected, is at the right side of the All Puissant, who represents Jehovah. The sounding of the seventh trumpet, and the conducting of the candidate to the canopy, is a representation of the end of the world, and the glorification of true Masons at the right hand of God, having "passed through the *trials* of Freemasonry," and "washed their robes in their own blood!" If this is not Antichrist, what is?—*Compiler.*]

The editor also adds the following foot-note in explanation of the foregoing:—"Compare the foregoing with the fifth, sixth and seventh chapters of Revelation, and the reader will discover that the All Puissant represents Jehovah seated on the throne of heaven; also, the Lamb of God, opening the seven seals. The Senior Warden represents the strong angel proclaiming: "Who is worthy to open the book," &c. The *aged* brethren, and the four old men with bladders, the angels of God with power; and Masonry claiming its faithful servants as the servants of God, the 144,000 who were sealed in their foreheads, and of whom it is said, "These are they who were not defiled with women; for they are virgins. These are they which follow the Lamb," &c. See Rev 14th chapter.

The following ceremonies are performed in the "Knights of the Christian Mark," found in the same book as the preceding, pp. 168—170; or eighth edition, 188—190:

"The Knights come to order; the Senior Knight takes his seat; the candidate continues standing; the conductor brings a white robe, the Senior Knight says: 'Thus saith the Lord, he that believeth and endureth to the end shall overcome, and I will cause his iniquities to pass from him, and he shall dwell in my presence for ever and ever. Take away his filthy garments from him, and clothe him with a change of raiment. For he that overcometh, the same shall be clothed in white raiment, and his name shall be written in the book of life, and I will confess his name before my Father and His holy angels. He that hath an ear let him hear what the Spirit saith unto the true believer. Set ye a fair miter upon his head, place a palm in his hand, for he shall go in and out, and minister before me, saith the Lord of hosts; and he shall be a disciple of that rod taken from the branch of the stem of Jesse. For a branch has grown out of his root,

and the Spirit of the Lord hath rested upon it
the Spirit of his wisdom and might, and right-
eousness is the girdle of his loins, and faithful-
ness the girdle of his reins; and he stands as
an insignia to the people, and him shall the
Gentiles seek, and his rest shall be glorious.
Cause them that have charge over the city to
draw near, everyone with the destroying weap-
on in his hand.' The six grand ministers come
from the north with swords and shields. The
first is clothed in white, and has an ink-horn
by his side, and stands before the Invincible
Knight, who says: 'Go through the city; run
in the midst thereof, and smite; let not thine
eye spare, neither have pity; for they have
not executed my judgments with clean hands,
saith the Lord of hosts.' The candidate is
instructed to exclaim: 'Woe is me, for I am a
man of unclean lips, and my dwelling has been
in the tents of Kedar, and among the children
of Meshec.' Then he that has the ink-horn
by his side, takes a live coal with the tongs
from the altar, and touches the lips of the
candidate, and says: 'If ye believe, thine
iniquities shall be taken away, thy sins shall
be purged. I will that these be clean with
the branch that is given up before me. All
thy sins are removed, and thine iniquities blot-
ted out. For I have trodden the wine-press

alone, and with me was none of my people
for behold I come with dyed garments from
Bozrah, mighty to save. Refuse not, therefore,
to hearken; draw not away thy shoulders;
shut not thine ear that thou shouldst not
hear.' The six ministers now proceed as though
they were about to commence the slaughter,
when the Senior Knight says to him with the
ink-horn: 'Stay thine hand; proceed no further
until thou hast set a mark on those that are
faithful in the house of the Lord, and trust in
the power of his might. Take ye the signet,
and set a mark on the forehead of my people
that have passed through great tribulation, and
have washed their robes, and have made them
white in the blood of the Lamb, which was
slain from the foundation of the world.' The
minister takes the signet and presses it on the
candidate's forehead. He leaves the mark in
red letters, 'King of kings, and Lord of lords.'
[ Foot-note:—'The reader is requested to turn
to the following passages:—Isa. vi. 5—7. Ps
cxx. 5. Isa. xliii. 15, and lxiii. 1—3. Rev. viii.
2—14, and xix. 16, and xv. 3. Zech. iii. 7. Song
of Solomon viii. 6, 7. The impious perversion
of these passages is incapable of defense or
excuse.] The Minister opens the scroll, and
says: 'Sir Invincible Knight, the number of
the sealed is one hundred and forty-four

thousand.' The Invincible Knight strikes **four**, and all the knights stand before him. He says. 'Salvation belongeth to our God which sitteth upon the throne, and to the Lamb.' All the members fall on their faces, and say: 'Amen. Blessing, honor, glory, wisdom, thanksgiving and power, might, majesty, and dominion, be unto our God for ever and ever. Amen.' They all cast down crowns and palm branches, and rise up and say: 'Great and numberless are thy works, thou King of saints. Behold, the star which I laid before Joshua, on which is engraved seven eyes as the engraving of a signet, shall be set as a seal on thine arm, as a seal on thine heart; for love is stronger than death, many waters cannot quench it. If a man would give all the treasures of his house for love, he cannot obtain it; it is the gift of God through Jesus Christ our Lord.'"

The following is found in the Royal Arch degree, pp. 126, first edition, 137, eighth edition:

"Question.—'Are you a Royal Arch Mason?' Answer.—'*I am that I am.*'" [Note. "I AM THAT I AM, is one of the peculiar names of the Deity; and to use it as above, is, to say the least, taking the name of God in vain. How must the humble disciple of Jesus feel when constrained *thus* to answer the question, "Are you a Royal Arch Mason?"] L on Masonry, seventh edition

On pp. 154, 155, we have a description of a ceremony in the same degree, as follows: "The candidates next receive the obligation, travel the room, attend the prayer, travel again, and are shown a representation of the *Lord appearing to Moses from the burning bush.* This last is done in various ways. Sometimes an earthen pot is filled with earth, and green bushes set around the edge of it, and a candle in the center; and sometimes a stool is provided with holes about the edge, in which bushes are placed, and a bundle of rags or tow, saturated with oil of turpentine, placed in the center, to which fire is communicated. Sometimes a large bush is suspended from the ceiling, around the stem of which tow is wound wet with the oil of turpentine. In whatever way the bush is prepared, when the words are read, 'He looked and behold the bush burned with fire,' etc., the bandage is removed from the eyes of the candidate, and they see the fire in the bush; and at the words, 'Draw not nigh hither, put off thy shoes,' etc., the shoes of the candidate are taken off, and they remain in the same situation while the rest of the passage to the words, 'And Moses hid his face; for he was afraid to look upon God,' is read. The bandage is then replaced, and the candidates again travel about the room while the next passage of Scripture is read."

[Note. "This is frequently represented in this manner: When the person reading comes to that part where it says, 'God called to him out of the midst of the bush, and said,' etc., he stops reading, and a person behind the bush calls out, 'Moses, Moses.' The conductor answers, 'Here am I.' The person behind the bush then says: 'Draw not nigh hither; put off thy shoes from off thy feet, for the place whereon thou standest is holy ground.' His shoes are then slipped off. 'Moreover, I am the God of Abraham, and the God of Isaac, and the God of Jacob.' The person first reading then says: 'And Moses hid his face, for he was afraid to look upon God.' At these words the bandage is placed over the candidate's eyes."] And, if any persons will examine, and read the books through for themselves, in which these revelations are made, they will find that the higher degrees are replete with the same shocking and monstrous perversion of the Scriptures. Many of the most solemn passages in the Bible are selected, read in their lodges, repeated by their candidates, and applied in a manner too shocking to read.

Here you observe the candidate taking the Royal Arch degree, when asked if he is a

Royal Arch Mason, replies: "*I am that I am;*" which is represented in the Bible as being said by Jehovah himself. This answer was given by God to Moses when he inquired after the Divine name. God answered, "I AM THAT I AM." Just think! a Christian, when inquired of if he is a Royal Arch Mason, affirms of himself, "*I am that I am,*" taking to himself the name of the God of Israel.

Again, in this representation of the burning bush, the candidate is told to take off his shoes from off his feet, for the place on which he stands is holy ground; and then the Master of the lodge claims to be the God of Abraham, of Isaac, and of Jacob. Now how awfully profane and blasphemous is this!

Again, observe that that most solemn scene, depicted in the ninth chapter of Ezekiel, is misapplied in the most profane manner. Reader, the chapter is short; will you not take your Bible and read it?

So again, in those chapters in Revelation, the opening of the seals by the Son of God is misapplied, and profanely misrepresented. Just think! four aged men, with bladders filled with wind, are made to represent the four angels that hold the four winds from desolating the earth till the servants of God were sealed in their foreheads. What a shocking misapplication and misrepresentation do we find here And the cases are numerons in which, as I have said, the most solemn passages in the Word of God are used in their mummeries and childish ceremonies, in so shocking a manner that we can hardly endure to read them. I beg my Christian readers to examine these books for themselves, and then see what they think of the assertions of so many professors of religion, and even of professed Christian ministers, that "there is nothing in Freemasonry inconsistent with the religion of Jesus Christ!" I cannot imagine anything more directly calculated to bring the Word of God into contempt, than such a use of it in Masonic lodges. It is enough to make one's blood curdle in his veins to think that a Christian minister, or any Christian whatever, should allow himself to pass through such an abominable scene as is frequently represented in the degrees of Masonry:—multiplying their horrid oaths, heaping one imprecation upon another, gathering up from every part of the Divine oracles the most solemn and awful sayings of Jehovah, and applying them in a manner so revolting, that the scene must make a Christian's heart tremble, and his whole soul to loathe such proceedings.

In some of my numerous letters I am requested to quote the oaths entire. But this would be to rewrite a great part of the books in which Masonry is revealed. Some of these degrees have several different oaths to sustain them, filling several pages of the work. I can only give parts of these oaths, and must leave the readers to consult the books for themselves· which I beseech them to do.

## CHAPTER XI.

## FREEMASONRY IMPOSES ON THE IGNORANT.

IN what is called the "Sublime Degree of Master Masons" there are the following gross misrepresentations worthy of notice:

First, Hiram Abiff is represented as going daily into the Most Holy place for secret prayer; whereas the Bible representation is that no one was allowed to enter the Most Holy place, except the high priest. Neither Solomon nor Hiram were allowed to enter it. And the high priest was allowed to enter it only once a year, and that on the great day of atonement, "not without blood, which he offered first for himself and then for the errors of the people."

Again, this Hiram is represented in Masonry as having been murdered by three ruffians, who demanded of him the Master's word.

As he refused to give it, they murdered him, and buried him at a distance from Jerusalem, in a grave "six feet deep perpendicular," where he remained fourteen days.

Then, after a great deal of twaddle and misrepresentation in regard to the supposed circumstances of his murder and burial, Solomon is represented as raising him from this depth in the earth by the Master's grip, and that "upon the five points of fellowship," which are, "foot to foot, knee to knee, breast to breast, hand to back, and mouth to ear."

It is no wonder that infidel Masons should ridicule the credulity of professed Christian Masons in crediting such a ridiculous story as this.

Again, Masonry goes on to represent that, after Hiram was thus raised from this grave, six feet deep—"foot to foot, knee to knee, breast to breast, hand to back, and mouth to ear"—he was brought up to Jerusalem, and buried under the Most Holy place in King Solomon's Temple. I will quote from the lecture of this degree, as found in the seventh edition of Bernard, p. 81: "Question [speaking of the body].—What did they do with the body? Answer.—Raised it in a Masonic form, and carried it up to the temple for more decent interment. Q.—Where was it buried? A.—Under the Sanctum Sanctorum, or Holy of Holies, over which they erected a marble monument, with this inscription delineated thereon, A virgin weeping over a broken column, with a book open before her; in her right hand a sprig of cassia; in her left, an urn; Time standing behind her, with his hands infolded in the ringlets of her hair."

Now, observe, this burial was under the Most Holy place in King Solomon's Temple; and the marble monument was erected over it, and consequently must have been in the Most Holy place itself. Does not every careful reader of the Bible know that this is false? We have a minute description in the Bible of everything relating to the Most Holy place—its form, size, embellishments, and of every article of furniture there was in it. No such statue was ever there, and the whole story is a gross falsehood.

But let me quote a little further from this lecture, continuing on page 81: "Q.—What does a Master's lodge represent? A.—The Sanctum Sanctorum, or Holy of Holies of King Solomon's Temple. Q.—How long was the temple building? A.—Seven years; during which it rained not in the daytime, that the workmen might not be obstructed in their labor." This is a likely story! Is there anything of this kind in the Bible? And does anyone believe that a miracle of this kind could have been wrought without having been recorded in the Bible? But again: "Q.—What supported the temple? A.—Fourteen hundred and fifty-three columns, and two thousand one hundred and six pilasters, all hewn from the finest Parian marble." Where did they get this? Again: "Q.—What further supported it? A.—Three grand columns or pillars. Q.—What were they called? A.—Wisdom, Strength, and Beauty. Q.—What did they represent? A.—The pillar of Wisdom represented Solomon, King of Israel, whose wisdom contrived the mighty fabric." But the Bible represents Solomon as having received the whole plan of the temple from David, who received it directly from God. Solomon never contrived the building at all.—1 Chon., xxviii. 11, 12, 20.

Again, on page 82, we have the following: " Q.—How many constitute a Master's lodge? A.—Three Master Masons. Q.—Where did they usually meet? A.—In the sanctum sanctorum, or Holy of holies of King Solomon's Temple." Now, this misrepresentation is kept up; and in the work of making a Master Mason they make the lodge represent the Most Holy place in King Solomon's Temple. A Masonic lodge in the Most Holy place of King Solomon's Temple! What an absurd, unscriptural, and ridiculous representation is this! And yet this is seriously taught to the candidate whenever a Master Mason is made.

But, again, this whole representation in regard to Hiram Abiff is utterly false. If any one will examine the fourth chapter of 2 Chron he will see that Hiram Abiff finished the work for which he was employed; and, so far as we can get any light from the Bible, he must have lived till after the temple was finished. Where and when he died we know not, as he, no doubt, returned to Hiram, King of Tyre, who sent him to assist Solomon. But that he died in the manner represented by Freemasons, that he was buried in a grave six feet deep, and raised upon the five points of fellowship, that he was then buried again under the Most Holy place of King Solomon's Temple, and a marble monument erected in the Most Holy place to his memory, is a glaring falsehood.

Again, Masonry teaches that the Master's word could only be given by three persons standing in a peculiar attitude, and each one repeating one of its syllables. That this word was known at the time by only three persons, Solomon, Hiram, King of Tyre, and Hiram Abiff; and that, consequently, when Hiram was killed, the word was lost, as they were under oath never to give it except in that particular manner.

Now, in the Royal Arch degree, Masonry professes to give an account of the manner in which that word was recovered.

Some men, it is said, were employed in digging about the temple, and discovered a stone, which proved to be the key-stone of an arch covering a vault deep under ground, constructed, as it is said, by Hiram Abiff, in which they found the Ark of the Covenant.

On pp. 78, 79, of Richardson's " Monitor of Freemasonry," we have their explanation of this pretended discovery as follows. On p. 78: " *Principal Sojourner.* — Most Excellent, in pursuance of your orders, we repaired to the secret vault and let down one of our companions. The sun at this time was at its meridian hight, the rays of which enabled him to discover a small box or chest standing on a pedestal, curiously wrought and overlaid with gold, \* \* \* We have brought this chest up for the examination of the Grand Council. *High Priest* [looking with surprise at the Ark].— Companion King this is the Ark of the Covenant of God. *King* [looking at it.]—It is un doubtedly the true Ark of the Covenant, Most Excellent. *High Priest* [taking the Ark].— Let us open it, and see what valuable treasure it may contain. [Opens the Ark, and takes out a book.] *High Priest to the King.*—Companion, here is a very ancient looking book. What can it be? Let us read it. [Reads the first three verses of the first chapter of Genesis.]"

After reading several other passages, the High Priest says: "This is a book of the law—long lost, but now found. Holiness to the Lord! [He repeats this twice]. *King.*—A book of the law—long lost, but now found. Holiness to the Lord! Scribe repeats the same. *High Priest to Candidates.*—You now see that the world is indebted to Masonry for the preservation of this sacred volume. Had it not been for the wisdom and precaution of our ancient brethren, this, the only remaining copy of the law, would have been destroyed at the destruction of Jerusalem." After several further misrepresentations, on p. 79, we have the following: "Looking again into the Ark, the High Priest takes out four pieces of paper, which he examines closely, consults with the king and scribe, and then puts them together so as to show a key to the ineffable characters of this degree. After examining the key, he proceeds to read by the aid of it the characters on the four sides of the Ark. High Priest reading first side: Deposited in the year three thousand. Second side: By Solomon, King of Israel. Third side: Hiram, King of Tyre, and Hiram Abiff. Fourth side: For the good of Masonry generally, but the Jewish nation in particular." If any one will consult the ceremonies just as they occur, and as they are recorded by Richardson, he will see to what an extent the candidate is misinformed and deceived in this degree. And the same in substance may be learned from "Light on Masonry." Now, observe, Masonry teaches in this most solemn manner that in Solomon's time the Ark of the Covenant, with its sacred contents, was buried in a vault by Solomon and the two Hirams.

Solomon was only the *third* king of Israel. And when did he have this Ark buried? Did it not stand in the Most Holy place during his own reign? Was not the Ark of the Covenant, with its sacred contents, in the Most Holy place in the temple after Solomon's day? What reader of the Bible does not *know* that this representation of Masonry is *false?* Again, the candidate is also falsely taught that the world is indebted to Masonry for preserving the book of the law; that, but for this discovery of the Ark with its contents in that vault, no book of the law would have been preserved, as this was the only copy in existence. But this, again, is utterly false. Masonry teaches that, but for the discovery of this volume, the Bible would have been lost at the destruction of Jerusalem. But there is no truth in this for copies had been multiplied before the first, and still further multiplied before the last, destruction of Jerusalem.

The following examples I extract from Professor Morgan's report: "It is alleged that, in consequence of the murder of Hiram Abiff, a particular keystone failed of its designation; but that Solomon caused search to be made for it, when it was found by means of certain initial letters which Hiram had employed as a mark. These letters were the initials of the English words, *H*iram, *T*yrian, *w*idow's *s*on *s*ent *t*o *K*ing *S*olomon. These initial letters are now employed as the *mark* of the Mark Master's degree. Masons sometimes wear a seal or trinket with these letters on it. I have seen them exhibited in a picture of a seal or badge in a widely circulated Masonic manual. Here we have Hiram, who never could have known one word of English—the English language not existing till thousands of years after his time—employing the initials of eight English words as his mark. And, in honor of his employing them, Mark Masters display them as their mark, and thus display the ignorance or imposture of their craft."

Another alleged historic fact is given in Richardson's "Monitor of Freemasonry," p. 155—the Gold Plate story. "In the ceremonies con nected with the degree of 'Grand Elect, Perfect, and Sublime Mason,' the Master says: 'I will now give you the true pronunciation of the name of the Deity as revealed to Enoch; and he engraved the letters composing it on a triangular plate of gold, which was hidden for many ages in the bowels of the earth, and lost to mankind. The mysterious words which you received in the preceding degrees are all so many corruptions of the true name of God which was engraved on the triangle of Enoch. In this engraving the *vowel points are so arranged as to give the pronunciation thus*, YOWHO. This word, when thus pronounced, is called the Ineffable word, which cannot be altered as other words are; and the degrees are called, on this account, Ineffable degrees. This word, you will recollect, was not found until after the death of Hiram Abiff; consequently, the word engraved by him on the ark is not the true name of God.'

"Here we have a most ridiculous piece of imposture, more than parallel with the gold plate imposture of Mormonism. Every Hebrew scholar of the most moderate attainments knows that the *vowel points*, here alleged to have been used by Enoch before the flood, did not even exist till six or eight centuries after the birth of Christ. Besides, the merest smatterer in Hebrew, with very little thought, would know that the name of God could not, by any proper arrangement of vowels, be pronounced in this way.

"The story could impose only on the grossest ignorance, or most careless inconsiderateness."

To quote all that is scandalously false in its teachings and pretensions would be to quote these books almost entire. We hear professed Christians, and even ministers, claiming that Freemasonry enables them to better understand the Bible. Can it be that they are so ignorant as to believe this? But this is often urged as an inducement to join the lodge. Indeed Masonry claims that, to this day, none but Freemasons know even the *true name of God*. After Enoch's day, the Divine name was unknown until recovered by Freemasons in the days of Solomon, and that this true name of God is preserved by them as a *Masonic secret*. Of course, all others are worshiping they know not what. So this is Masonic benevolence and piety, to conceal from all but their craft the name of the true God. How wise and benevolent Freemasonry is! I wonder how many ministers of the Gospel are engaged in keeping this secret! They only of all ministers know the true name of God, and have joined a conspiracy to conceal it from all but Masons!

Before I close this number, I wish to ask Freemasons who have taken the degrees above the Fellow craft, or second degree, have you believed the teaching of these degrees, as you have taken them one after another? Have you believed that the lodges, chapters, commanderies, etc., were really erected to God, and consecrated to the holy order of Zerubbabel and St. John? Have you believed what you are taught in the Master's degree, respecting King Solomon, Hiram, king of Tyre, and Hiram Abiff? Have you believed the teachings of the Royal Arch degree, and of all those degrees in which King Solomon figures so largely? Have you believed that to Masonry the church owes the preservation of the only remaining copy of the law of God? Have you believed the Gold Plate story, that Enoch lived in the place where the Temple of Solomon was afterward built, that he built, deep in the earth, nine arches, one above the other, in which, on the place where the temple was afterward built, he deposited a golden plate on which was written the true name of God, that this name was written with the Hebrew vowels attached, and that its true pronunciation is YOWHO, as Masonry teaches? Now you *have*

believed these, and other outrageous falsehoods
taught in Masonry, or you have *not*. If you
have believed them, you have been greatly
imposed upon, you have been grossly deceived.
Will you allow yourselves to still give countenance to an institution that teaches such falsehoods as these? Had I space I could fill scores
of pages with the palpable falsehoods which
Masonry teaches its membership. How can
you adhere to an institution so basely false and
hypocritical as this? The secrets are all out.
Both you and the world are now made aware
of the base falsehoods that are palmed off upon
its members by Freemasonry. Professed Christian Freemason, how can you hold up your head
either in the church or before the world, if you
still adhere to this most hypocritical institution!
Just think of the Worshipful Masters, the Grand
High Priests, in their mitres and priestly robes,
the great and pompous dignitaries of Masonry
arrayed in *their* sacerdotal robes, solemnly
teaching their members such vile falsehoods as
these, claiming that to Freemasons the church
owes the preservation of the law of God, and
that the true name of God is known only to
Freemasons! Shame! But I said you have
either been made to believe these things or
you have not. If you have never believed
them, pray, let me ask you how it is that you

have ever given any countenance to this institution when you did not at all believe its teaching? How is it that you have not long since renounced and denounced an institution whose teaching is replete with falsehoods taught under the most solemn circumstances? These falsehoods are taught as Masonic secrets, under the sanction of the most awful and solemn oaths. What shall we say of an institution that binds its members by such oaths, to keep and preserve as truth and secrets, such a tissue of profane falsehood? You see nothing in it inconsistent with Christianity! Why, my dear brother, how amazing it is that you can be so blinded! Are you not afraid that you shall be given over to believe a lie, that you may be damned, because you believe not the truth, but have **pleasure in unrighteousness**

## CHAPTER XII.
## MASONRY SUSCEPTIBLE OF CHANGE ONLY BY ADDITIONS.

IN proof of this, I first appeal to the testimony of Masons themselves. Hear the testimony, given under oath, of Benjamin Russell, once Grand Master of the Grand Lodge of Massachusetts. His and other depositions were given in Boston, before a justice of the peace, by request of Masons themselves. Observe, he was an ex-Grand Master of one of the most important lodges in the world. This surely is conclusive Masonic authority. He says: "*The Masonic institution has been, and now is, the same in every place. No deviation has been made, or can be made at any time, from its usages, rules and regulations.*" Observe, he does not say that no *additions* can be made, but no *deviatons*. He proceeds: "Such is its nature, that no innovations on its customs can be introduced, or sanctioned, by any person or persons. DeWitt Clinton, the former Governor of New York and

Grand Master of the Grand Lodge of New York and of the United States, also made an affidavit on the same occasion. He says: "*The priniples of Masonry are essentially the same and uniform in every place*" (Powell, p. 40, as quoted by Stearns). In Hardy's Monitor, a standard Masonic work, we have the following, p. 96: "*Masonry stands in no need of improvement; any attempt, therefore, to introduce the least innovation will be reprobated, not by one, but by the whole fraternity.*" The Grand Lodge of Connecticut asserts: "It is not in the power of man, nor in any body of men, to remove the ancient landmarks of Masonry" (Allyn's Ritual, p. 14). These are the highest Masonic authorities, and to the same effect might be quoted from all their standard works.

Second.—From the nature of the institution it cannot be changed, except by addition. In proof of this I observe

I. That Masonry is extended over the civilized world, at least Masons themselves boast that it includes men of every language, and of every clime. They claim for Masonry that it is a universal language; that men of every country and language can reveal themselves to each other as Freemasons; that by their signs and grips and pass words, etc., they can not only know each other as Masons, but as having taken such and such degrees of the order. that as soon as they reveal themselves to each other as having taken certain degrees of Masonry, they know their obligations, each to the other—what they may demand or expect of each other, and what each is under oath to do for the other. Now this must be true, or of what avail would Masonry be to those who are traveling through different countries, where there are different languages. Unless their methods of knowing each other were uniform, universal, and unchangable, it is plain that they could not know each other as Masons. It is true in some particular localities there may be an additional pass word or sign, to indicate that they belong to *that locality*, but in all that is essentially Masonic, it must be universal and unchangable.

II. The same is true with respect to their oaths. They must all, in every place, be under the same obligations to each other, or it would introduce endless confusion and uncertainty. Every Mason, of every place, must know that every other Mason, having taken the same degrees, has taken the same oaths that he himself has taken; that he owes the same duties, and can claim the same privileges of any other Mason of the same degree. If this were not so, Masonry would be of no value among strangers. Furthermore, if their obligations were not exactly alike, they would necessarily be betrayed into violating them. If they found that they claimed duties of each other which were not necessarily imposed by the obligations of both, or claimed privileges of each other not conferred by the obligations of both, they would in this way make each other acquainted with their respective obligations which were not in fact alike. Thus each would reveal to the other, secrets which he was sworn to keep.

III. The oaths of every degree, from the lowest to the highest, must be uniform, everywhere the same, and unchangable. If they were not the same in every country, in every language, and at every time, Masonry would be a perfect babel. New degrees may be added *ad infinitum*, but a Mason of any degree must know that Masons of the same degree in every place, have taken the same oath that he has taken, and have taken all the oaths of the previous degrees, just as he has himself. If this were not true, Masons could not everywhere know with what they might entrust each other. Suppose, for example, that the obligation to conceal each other's crimes, and to keep each other's secrets, was not universal and unchangeable, how would they know with what they might trust each other in different places? Suppose the obligation to assist each other in getting out of any difficulty, whether right or wrong, was not uniform and universal, how would they know what they might demand of, or were under obligation to perform for, each other? But can not its objectionable points, it may be asked, be dropped out, and what is valuable preserved? Drop from the obligation, for instance, in any place, the clause that binds them to keep each other's secrets, murder and treason excepted, or without exception,—to deliver each other from difficulty, whether right or wrong, to give each other precedence in business or politics, to give each other warning of any approaching danger and the like. Now if you drop out any one of these, at any time or place, you introduce confusion, and Masons could not understand each other. Furthermore, drop out the most objectionable features of Masonry, and you have robbed it of its principal value to the membership, you have annihilated the principal reasons for becoming and for remaining a Mason. But the changes are manifestly impossible. There is nowhere any authority for such change; and, as has been stated, the whole fraternity would rebuke any attempt at such innovation. We may rest assured, therefore, that Freemasonry is not.

and can not be, essentially changed, except by addition. To this point all their highest authorities bear the fullest testimony. Its very *nature* forbids essential innovations at any time or in any place. But should Masons affirm that the institution is changed, how are we to know what changes have been made? They are under oath to keep this a profound secret. Suppose they were to affirm that, since the revelations made by Morgan, Bernard, and others, the institution has been greatly improved, this is a virtual admission that those books are true, which they have so often denied. But since they have first denied that those books were true, and now virtually admit their truth, by claiming that Masonry has been improved since those books were written, what reason have we to believe them? I have, in a previous number, shown that it is irrational to believe what Masons themselves say in respect to their secrets. I do not know that any intelligent and respectable Freemason pretends that Masonry has been improved. But suppose they should, how shall we know in what respects it has been improved, that we may judge for ourselves whether the changes *are* improvements. If any number of them were now to affirm that Masonry, as it now exists, is divested of all the objectionable features that formerly belonged to it, how shall we know whether this is true?— They have always denied that it *had* any objectionable features; they have always claimed that it needed no improvement, and their highest authorities have many times affirmed that all improvement and innovation were impossible. In view of all the testimony in the case, we have no right to believe that Masonry is at all improved from what it was forty years ago. As late as 1860, Richardson revealed sixty-two degrees of Masonry as it then existed. It was then the same in every essential feature as when Bernard made his revelation in 1829, and when Avery Allyn made his revelation in 1831. We are all, therefore, under the most solemn obligations to believe that Masonry is, in all important particulars, just what is has been since its various degrees have been adopted and promulged. We certainly do greatly err and sin, if, in view of all the facts, we assume, and act upon the assumption, that Freemasonry is divested of its immoral and obnoxious features. Such an assumption is utterly unwarranted, because, on the one hand, there is no evidence of the fact, and, on the other, there is positive and abundant proof that no such change has been made. We are all, therefore, responsible to God and to humanity for the course we shall take respecting the institution. We are bound to judge of it, and to treat it, according to the evidence in the case, which is, that *Freemasonry is necessarily a wicked institution, and incapable of thorough moral reformation.*

I have spoken frequently of its having the character, in certain respects, of a mutual aid, or mutual insurance, company. It is inquired, are all these necessarily wicked? I answer, no. The benefits of these institutions may be real and great. For example, an insurance company that insures persons against loss by shipwreck, by fire, or by what we call accident of any kind, may be very beneficial to society. When they help each other in cases of calamity that involve no crime, they are not necessarily wicked, but may be very useful. The benefits of these companies are open to all upon reasonable conditions; and if any do not reap the fruits of them, it is not the fault of the society, but of those who neglect to avail themselves of its benefits. But Freemasonry is by no means a *mere* insurance or mutual aid society. The moral character of any institution must depend on the *end* at which it aims;—that is, the moral character of any society *is found in the end* it is intended to secure. Mutual aid and insurance companies, as they exist for business purposes, do not necessarily deprive any one of his rights, and are often highly useful. The members of such societies or companies do not know each other, nor exert over each other any *personal* influence whatever. They are not bound by any oath to render each other any unlawful assistance, to conceal each other's crimes, nor "to espouse each other's cause, whether right or wrong." There is no clannish spirit engendered by their frequent meeting together, nor by mutual pledges under the most awful oaths and penalties, to treat each other with any favoriteism under any circumstances. But Freemasonry, on the contrary, does pledge its members by the most solemn oaths, to aid each other in a manner that sets aside the rights of others. For example, they are sworn first, in the Master's degree, to conceal each other's crimes, "murder and treason only excepted;" second, in the Royal Arch degree, "murder and treason not excepted;" in this same degree they swear to endeavor to extricate each other, if involved in any difficulty, whether they are right or wrong; third, they also swear to promote each other's political elevation in preference to any one of equal qualifications who is not a Freemason; fourth, to give each other the preference in business transactions.—See Richardson's Monitor of Freemasonry, p. 92. Degree of Secret Monitor: "I furthermore promise and swear, that I will caution a brother Secret Monitor by signs, word, or token, whenever I see him doing, or about to do, any thing contrary to his interest in buying or selling. I furthermore promise and swear, that I will assist a brother Secret Monitor in preference to any other person by introducing him to business, by sending him custom, or in *any other manner* in which I can throw a penny in his way." They swear "to represent all who violate their Masonic oaths as worthless vagabonds, and to send this character after them to ruin their business and their reputation wherever they may go and be to the end of their lives." They also swear to seek the condign punishment of all such in the infliction of the penalties of their oaths upon them. They swear to *seek their death.* They swear to a stringent exclusiveness, excluding from their society all that would most naturally need aid and sympathy, and receiving none who are not "physically perfect." Old men in dotage, young men in nonage, all women, idiots and other needy classes, are all excluded. Freemasonry has a vast fund of money at its disposal. The fraternity are very numerous. They boast of numbering in this country at the present time six hundred thousand, and that they are multiplying faster than ever. They permeate every community, and their influence is almost omnipresent. Of course, such an aid society as this will everywhere and in every thing ignore and trample on the rights of others to secure advantages for each other. As an illustration of the workings of this society, I make an extract or two from "The American Freemason," published in Louisville, Kentucky, dated April 8, 5854, that is 1854, and edited by Robert Morris, an eminent Masonic author. From the eighty-fifth page I quote as follows: "Lynn, Indiana.—In hauling a load of pork to the depot a year or two since, I found the rush of wagons so great that the delivery was fully three days behind. This was a serious matter to me, for I could not lose so much time from my business, and was seriously weighing the propriety of going on to Cincinnati with my load, when the freight agent, learning from a casual remark of mine, that I was a Freemason, was kind enough at once to order my errand attended to, and in three hours I was unloaded, and ready, with a light heart, to set my face homeward. Is it not an admirable thing, this Masonic spirit of brotherly love?" To this the editor adds: "Verily it is. We have seen it in many varieties of form, but our kind-hearted brother's is but an every-day experience of Masonic practice, but to the world how inexplicable do such things appear." Here we have a specimen of Masonic brotherly love. But was this right, to give this preference to this man, and wrong all who were there before him, and had a right to have their business done before him! He gained three days' time, and saved the expense of waiting for his turn, whilst others were obliged to lose both the time and expense. And this we are coolly told, by high Masonic authority, is the "constant practice of Freemasons." What an exquisite brotherly love is this. It is delicious! But this is in entire accordance with the spirit of their oaths. But is it not a trampling on the rights of others! In this same paper we have, in an illustration of the nature of Freemasonry, a tale, the substance of which is, that a criminal, under sentence of death, was set free by Freemasons under the pretense that he was not guilty of the murder for which he was condemned. So they took the case into their own hands, and set aside the judgment of the court and jury. Observe, this is given as an illustration of the manner in which Freemasons aid each other

These cases are given as their own boast of specimens of their brotherly love. But is this consistent with right and good government? The fact is, that it is impossible to engage in any business, to travel, to do any thing, to go anywhere, without feeling the influence of this and other secret societies. Wrongs are constantly inflicted upon individuals and upon society, of which the wronged are unaware. We can be wronged any day by a favoritism practiced by these societies, without being aware how or by whom we are wronged. I was informed of late, that in a large manufacturing establishment, poor men, dependent for their daily bread upon their labors in the factory, were turned out to give place to Freemasons who were no better workmen than themselves. Indeed it is inevitable that such a society should act upon such a principle. But it may be asked, can not Masonry be *essentially reformed*, so that it shall involve no wrong? I answer, no, unless its very fundamental principle and aim be reversed, and then it would cease to be Freemasonry. In its workings it is a constant wrong inflicted upon society. It is an incessant and wide-spread conspiracy for the concealment of crime, to obstruct the course of justice, and, in many instances, to persecute the innocent and let the wicked go free. To reform it, its ends and its means must both be reformed. It must cease to be exclusive and selfish. It must cease to promise aid in many forms in which it does promise it. I have said that it was more than an innocent mutual aid society. Its members are pledged to aid each other in concealing iniquity, and in many ways that trample upon the rights of others.

And it is because this society promises aid in so many ways, and under so many circumstances, that men unite themselves to it. I have never heard any better reason assigned for belonging to it, than that, in many respects, one might reap a *personal advantage* from it. Now reform it, and make it a truly benevolent society; reform out of it all unrighteous favoritism, and all those forms of aid which are inconsistent with the universal good, and the highest well-being of society in general, and you have altered its essential nature; it is no longer Freemasonry, or any thing like Freemasonry. To *reform* it is to *destroy* it. In this view of Freemasonry, it is easy to see how difficult, if not impossible, it is for a man to be a consistent Freemason and yet a Christian. Just conceive of a Christian constantly receiving the preference over others as good as himself, in traveling, in railroad cars, on steamboats, at hotels, and everywhere, and in business transactions, and in almost all the relations of life, allowing himself to be preferred to others who have equal rights with himself. To be sure, in traveling, he may bless himself because he is so comfortable, and that so much pains are taken to give him the preference in every thing. If at a hotel, he may have the best seat at the table, and the best room in the house, and may find himself everywhere more favored than others.

But can he honestly accept this? Has he any right to accept it? No, indeed, he has not! He is constantly favored at the expense of others. He constantly has more than his right, while others are deprived of their rights. In other words, he is selfish, and that continually. He finds a *personal benefit* in it. Yes, and that is why he adheres to it. But again, if true to his oath, he is not only thus constantly *receiving* benefits unjustly, or to the injury of others, but also *conferring* them.

Whenever he sees a Masonic sign and recognizes a Masonic brother, he, of course, must do by him as a Freemason, as he himself is done by.

How can a man who is a Christian allow himself to be influenced by such motives as are presented in Freemasonry? Now let it be understood that all action is to be judged by its motive. No man has a right to receive or confer favors that interfere with the rights of others. And a man who can travel about the country and make himself known as a Freemason for the purpose of being indulged, and finding the best place in a hotel, or the best seat in a railroad car, or the best state-room in a steamboat, must be a selfish man, and can not be a Christian,—for a selfish man is not a Christian. Let it then be understood that Masonry in its fundamental principle, in which its moral character is found, is not reformed, and can not be reformed without destroying its very nature.

It can not be a part of general benevolence but stands unalterably opposed to the highest well-being of society in general. The same, let me say, is true to a greater or less extent of all secret societies, whose members are bound by oath or pledge to treat each other with a favoritism that ignores the rights of others. Now, it has been said, and I think truly, that in the late war if a man wished preferment and high rank, he must be a high Mason. Such things were managed so much by high Masons that it was difficult for a man to rise in rank unless he could make himself known as a high Mason. And let the facts become known—and, *I hope that measures will be taken to make them known*—and I believe it will be found that the great mass of the lucrative offices in the United States are in the hands of the Freemasons.

It is evident that they are aiming to seize upon the government, and to wield it in their own interest. They are fast doing this, and unless the nation awake soon it will be too late. And let the church of God also awake to the fact that many of her ministers and members are uniting with a society so selfish and wicked as this, and are defending it, and are ready to persecute all who will not unite with them in this thing. What Mr. Morris said of the nature of Freemasonry, that is, that it was the constant practice of Freemasons to give each other the preference, as in the case of the man delivering his load, is really what every observant man, especially if he has ever been himself a Mason, knows to be true.

When Freemasons say that it is "a good thing," they mean by this that men reap personal advantage from it. But I am bound to say, that I should feel utterly ashamed to have any one offer to give me a right that belonged to others because I was a Mason.

It has been frequently said, by persons: "If I was going to travel, I would become a Freemason." A physician in the United States Army in the late war, said to a relative of his: "If I were going into the army again, I would be sure to become a Freemason. There is such a constant favoritism shown by Freemasons to each other, on every occasion, that were I going to take the field again, I would be sure to avail myself of the benefits of that institution." Now, in opposition to this, I would say, that were I going to travel, or were I going to enlist in the army, I should be *ashamed* to avail myself of any such benefits at all. It is not right that any such favoritism should exist, and any man ought to reject with indignation the proposal of such favoritism. Any man should blush, if he has entertained the thought of allowing himself to be placed in such a selfish position. But it is asserted, no doubt with truth, that oftentimes the lives of brother Masons have been spared, simply because of this relation. But shall a man save his life by wrong-doing? He had better remember, that if he attempts this, he ruins his own soul. He that would thus "save his life, shall lose it." A man can gain nothing in the end by wrong-doing; let him do *right*, and if, by so doing, he loses his life, he will be sure to save it. With my present knowledge of Freemasonry I would not become a Freemason to save my life a thousand times

## CHAPTER XIII.

## THE CLAIM OF FREEMASONRY TO GREAT ANTIQUITY IS FALSE.

WE have seen that Freemasonry has been truly revealed. We have examed its *oaths, principles, claims,* and teaching, so far as to prepare the way for an examination of its moral character and tendencies, and also its relations to both Church and State. This I now proceed to do. And

1. *Its claims to great antiquity are false.* Every one at all acquainted with the claims of Freemasonry knows that it professes to have existed in the days of Solomon; and it is claimed that Solomon himself was a Freemason, and that John the Baptist and John the Evangelist were Freemasons. Indeed, the writers frequently trace it back as coeval with the creation itself. Masons have claimed for their institution an antiquity antecedent to human government; and from this they have argued that they aave a right to execute the penalties of their oaths, because Masonry is older than govern-

ment. Now an examination will show that this claim is utterly false. Their own highest authorities *now* pronounce it to be false; and still these claims are kept up, and their oaths and ceremonies, and the whole structure of the institution profess the greatest antiquity.

Solomon, for instance, figures as a Freemason everywhere in their ceremonies.

Their lodges are dedicated to St. John; and in the third degree there is a scene professed to have been enacted in the temple and at the building of the Temple of Solomon.

Now, all this is utterly fallacious, a false pretense, and a swindle; because it is the obtaining of money from those who join them under false pretenses.

Steinbrenner, a great Masonic historian, after much research, with manifest candor, says that Speculative Freemasonry—which is the only form of Freemasonry now existing—dates no further back than 1717. The article on Freemasonry in the new "American Encyclopedia" agrees with this statement of Steinbrenner. Indeed, all modern research on this subject has resulted in dating the commencement of Freemasonry, as it now exists, not far from the middle of the eighteenth century.

Dr. Dalcho, the compiler of the book of constitutions for South Carolina, says: "*Neither*

*Adam, nor Noah, nor Nimrod, nor Moses, nor Joshua, nor David, nor Solomon, nor Hiram, nor St. John the Baptist, nor St. John the Evangelist, were Freemasons. Hypothesis in history is absurd. There is no record, sacred or profane, to induce us to believe that those holy men were Freemasons; and our traditions do not go back to those days. To assert that they were Freemasons may make the vulgar stare, but will rather excite the contempt than the admiration of the wise."*

Now, observe, this is a high authority, and should be conclusive with Masons, because it is one of their own leaders who affirms this. But, if this is true, what shall we think of the claims of Freemasonry itself? For every one who reads these revelations of Freemasonry will see that Solomon, and Hiram, and those ancient worthies everywhere figure in these rites and ceremonies; so that, if these men were indeed not Masons, then Freemasonry is a sham, an imposture, and a swindle. What! has it come to this, that this boasted claim of antiquity, which everywhere lies at the foundation of Masonic rites, ceremonies, and pretensions, is now discovered to be false!

Through all the Masonic degrees the presense is kept up that Masonry has always been one and the same; and that its degrees are ancient, and all its principles and usages of great antiquity. Let any one examine the books in which it is revealed, and he can not help being struck with this. Furthermore, in the orations, sermons, and puffs that are so common with Masons on all occasions on which they show themselves off, they flaunt their very ancient date, their very ancient principles and usages, and they pledge their candidates, from one degree to another, to conform to all the ancient rites, principles, and usages of the order.

But what shall we at the present day say of these pretensions? I have before me the *Masonic Monthly* for October, 1867, printed in Boston. It will not be denied, I suppose, that this is one of their standard authorities. At any rate, whatever may be said of the editor of this paper, it will not be denied that the authorities quoted in the discussions in this number are high, if not the very highest authorities in the Masonic fraternity. If I had space to quote nearly this entire number, I should be very happy to do so, for it is occupied almost entirely, from beginning to end, with exposing these pretensions to which I have alluded. It appeals to their own standard authorities; and insists that Speculative Freemasonry, in all its higher degrees, is an imposture and a swindle.

It quotes their great historian—Steinbrenner, of New York—to show that Speculative Freemasonry was first established in London, in 1717; and that at that time Masonry consisted probably, of but *one* degree. That about 1725 a Mr. Anderson added two degrees; and, as the writer in this number states, began the *Christianizing* of Freemasonry. There is at this day a great division among Freemasons themselves, the point of disagreement being this: One party maintains that the Christian religion is of no more authority with Masons than any other form of religion; that Masonry proper does not recognize the Bible as of any higher authority than the sacred books of heathen nations, or than the Koran of Mohammed; that Freemasonry proper recognizes all religions as equally valid, and that so far as Masonry is concerned it matters not at all what the religion of its adherents is, provided they be not Atheists. The other party maintains that Masonry is founded upon the Bible, and that it is substantially a Christian institution.

This controversy is assuming extensive proportions, and it is very interesting for outsiders to look into it. I say *outsiders*—and I might say it is important, and would be very creditable, for the members of the fraternity to un-

derstand this matter better than they do; for
I doubt if one in twenty of them is posted in
regard to the real state of this question among
the fraternity themselves. Mr. Evans, who is
the editor of this *Masonic Monthly*, takes the
ground, and I think sustains it fully from their
own authorities, that all the upper degrees of
Masonry are an imposture.

He goes on to show where and by whom, in
several important cases, these upper degrees
were manufactured and palmed off on the
brotherhood as ancient Freemasonry.

For example, he shows that Mr. Oliver, one
of their most prolific authors, asserts that one
of the grand lodges in London gave charters,
about the middle of the eighteenth century,
to the Masonic lodges in France; and that in
France they immediately betook themselves
to manufacturing degrees and palming them
off on the public as of very ancient origin.
They proceeded to manufacture a thousand of
these degrees in France. Many of them they
asserted they had received from Scotland; but
the Grand Lodge of Scotland denied ever having known of those degrees.

It is also asserted in this number that the
Royal Arch degree was at first but an appendage to a Master's lodge, and had no separate
charter, and for a long time was not recognized

at all as any part of Freemasonry. And it informs us when and by whom the Royal Arch degree was manufactured. This number also shows that many of the Masonic degrees have originated in Charleston, South Carolina; and that a man by the name of Webb, in Massachusetts, manufactured the Templars' degrees. In short, we find here their own standard authorities showing up all the higher degrees of Masonry as having been gotten up and palmed off on the fraternity in order to make money out of them; and is not this a swindle? I wish to call the attention especially of the fraternity to these statements in this number of the *Masonic Monthly*.

Indeed, it is now common for the highest and best informed Masons to ridicule the pretense that Speculative Freemasonry is an ancient institution, as a humbug and a lie, having no foundation in correct history at all. Now will Freemasons examine this subject for themselves?—for they have been imposed upon.

I am particularly anxious to have professed Christians who are Freemasons thoroughly understand this matter. They have regarded Freemasonry as entirely consistent with the Christian religion, and have professed to see in it nothing with which a Christian can not have fellowship. In the third, or Master's, degree we find the story of Hiram Abiff introduced into Masonry.

Now this number of the *Monthly* charges, that this class of Freemasons went on to construct all the subsequent degrees of Freemasonry from the Bible, by ransacking the whole Old and New Testaments for striking passages from which they could construct new degrees, thus leaving the impression that Masonry was a divine institution, and founded upon the Bible.

If professed Christians who are Freemasons will really examine this subject, they will see that a Masonic lodge is no place for a Christian.

But suppose it should be asked, may we not innocently take those degrees that are founded upon the Bible, and that recognize the Christian religion as of divine authority? I answer, Christians cannot be hypocrites. Let it be distinctly understood, that all these higher degrees are shown to be an imposture; and that this Christianizing of Freemasonry has consisted in heaping up a vast mass of falsehood, and of palming it off upon the fraternity as truth and as ancient Freemasonry.

Can Masonic orators be honest in still

claiming for Speculative Masonry great antiquity, divine authority, and that it is a saving institution? Masons are themselves now showing that the whole fabric of Speculative Freemasonry is an enormous falsehood Stone Masonry, doubtless, had its simple degree, and its pass words and signs by which they knew each other. It also had its obligations. But upon that little stem have been engrafted a great number of spurious and hypocritical degrees.

This does seem to be undeniable. Now will Freemasons be frank enough to acknowledge this, and to say frankly that they have been imposed upon? Will they come out from all fellowship with such an imposture and such a swindle?

It has then come at last to this, that the highest authority among Freemasons has taken the ground that the Freemasonry which has been so eulogized throughout the length and breadth of the land, and which has drawn in so many professed Christians and ministers, is nothing less than an enormous cheat. That those behind the curtain, who have manufactured and sold these degrees—those Grand Chapters and Encampments and Commanderies, and all those pompous assemblies—have been engaged in enticing the brotherhood who had taken the lower degrees, to come up into their ranks and pay their money, that they may line their pockets. Now remember that these positions are fully sustained by Masons themselves, as their views are set forth in this number of the *Masonic Monthly.*

I do most earnestly entreat Freemasons to inform themselves on this subject; and not turn around and tell us that they, being Freemasons, know more about it than we do ourselves. The fact is, my friends, many of you do not. You do not read. I have myself recently conversed with a Freemason who admitted to me that he was entirely ignorant of what was being said in Masonic periodicals on this subject. I do not believe that one in twenty of the Masonic fraternity in this country is aware of the intense hypocrisy with which all the higher degrees of Masonry have been palmed off upon them, and upon the whole fraternity. Can men of honor and of principle allow their names and influence to be used to sustain such an enormous mass of false pretension?

But again, no one can read Bernard on Masonry through, or any of these authors, without perceiving the most unmistakable evidence that most of the degrees in Masonry are of modern date. I do not know why so much stress should be laid upon the antiquity of Masonry by those who embrace and adhere to it. It surely does not prove that it is of any value, or that it is true. Sin is of very ancient date, heathenism is of very ancient date, and most of the abominations that are in the world are of very ancient date; but this is no reason for embracing them, or regarding them as of any great importance.

But to certain minds there is a charm in the appearance and profession of antiquity; and *young* Masons are universally deceived in this respect, and led to believe that it is one of the most ancient of existing institutions, if not the very most so. Now I would not object to Masonry because it is of modern origin; for this would not prove it to be false, if it did not profess to be of *ancient* origin. I notice this false pretense not because I think its being of recent date would prove it unworthy of notice, or of immoral character or tendency. But observe that its pretensions from first to last are that it is of very ancient date; and it is traced back to the days of inspiration, and is claimed to have been founded and patronized by inspired men.

What would Masonry be if all its claims to antiquity were stricken out, and if those degrees in Masonry, and those ceremonies and usages, were abolished that rest upon the claim that Solomon, that Hiram Abiff, and John the Evangelist, were Freemasons? What would remain of Freemasonry if all those claims found in the very *body* of the institution were stricken out? Why, their very lodges are dedicated to the holy order of St. John and Zerubbabel, etc. But what had St. John to do with Freemasonry? Manifestly nothing. He never heard or thought of it. Nor did Solomon or Zerubbabel.

And here let me say a word to young men who have been urged to unite with this fraternity, and who have been made to believe that the institution is so very ancient that it was established and patronized by those holy men. My dear young men, you have been deceived. You have been imposed upon as I was imposed upon. You have been made to believe a lie. They have drawn your money from you under false pretenses that some very ancient mysteries were to be revealed to you; and that the institution was one established as far back, at least, as the days of Solomon, and that St. John was the patron of the institution. Now this, rely upon it is but a pretense, a sham, an imposture, and a swindle. I beg you to believe me; and if you will examine the subject for yourselves, you will find it to be true.

Your own best historian, Steinbrenner, will teach you that Freemasonry, as you know it, and as it is now universally known, dates no further back than the eighteenth century. And Dr. Dalcho, who is good authority with the brotherhood, as we have seen, repudiates the idea of its antiquity as that which "may make the vulgar stare, but will rather excite the contempt than the admiration of the wise." I know that Masons affirm that the institution in its present form is the descendant of a brotherhood of stone masons, whose history may be traced back for some seven hundred years. But remember that Freemasonry, as you know it, and as it now exists, is not at all what it was among those simple artisans. The name is preserved, and some of its symbols, for the purpose of claiming for it great antiquity. But do not be deceived. If you will examine the subject for yourselves, you will find that modern Freemasonry is entirely another thing from that from which it claims to be descended. And when you hear ministers, or orators, on any occasion, claiming for Speculative Freemasonry—which is the only form in which it now exists—a great antiquity, let it be settled, I pray you, in your minds, that such claims are utterly false; and that those who make them are either grossly ignorant or intensely dishonest. *King Solomon a stone mason! Hiram a Grand Master of a Grand Lodge of stone masons! Those men uniting in a lodge with a company of stone masons!* Does any one really believe the silly tale?

How long shall the intelligent of this generation be insulted by having this pretended antiquity of Freemasonry paraded before the public? Do not intelligent Freemasons blush to hear their orators on public occasions, and even ministers of the Gospel in their Masonic sermons, flaunt the silly falsehoods of the great antiquity of Freemasonry before the public, and claim that Enoch, Zerubbabel, Solomon, the St. Johns, and all the ancient worthies, were Freemasons!

## CHAPTER XIV.
## THE BOASTED BENEVOLENCE OF FREE MASONS A SHAM.

THE law of God requires universal benevolence, supreme love to God, and equal love to our neighbor—that is, to all mankind.

This the Gospel also requires, and this is undeniable. But does *Masonry* inculcate this morality? and is this *Masonic benevolence?*

By no means. Masonic oaths require *partial* benevolence; or strictly, they require no benevolence at all. For real benevolence is universal in its own nature. It is good-willing; that is, it consists in willing the well-being or good of universal being—and that for its own sake, and not because the good belongs to this or that particular individual.

In other words, true benevolence is necessarily *impartial*. But Masonic oaths not only do not require impartial and universal benevolence, but they require the exact opposite of this. The law and Gospel of God allow and require us to discriminate in our *doing* good between the holy and the wicked.

They require us to do good, as we have opportunity, to all men, but *especially* to the household of faith. But the Masonic oaths make no such discriminations as this, nor do they allow it. These oaths require Masons to discriminate between Masons and those that are not Masons; giving the preference to Masons, even if they are not Christians, rather than to Christians if they are not Masons.

Now this is directly opposite to both the law and the Gospel. But this is the benevolence and morality of Freemasonry, undeniably.

The law and the Gospel require our discriminations in our treatment of men to be conditional upon their holiness and likeness to God and their faith in Jesus Christ.

But the oaths of Freemasons require their discriminations to be founded upon the mere relation of a brother Mason, whatever his Christian or moral character may be.

It is not pretended that a man may not be a good and worthy Mason who is not a Christian. It is admitted and claimed by Freemasonry that a man's religion, or *religious* character has nothing to do with his being a Mason. If he admits the being of a God this is enough.

Now this, I say again, is not only not in accordance with Christian morality, and with the law and Gospel of God; but it is directly opposed to both law and Gospel.

But, again, the utter want of true benevolence in the Masonic institution will further appear if we consider the *exclusiveness* of the institution. A minister in Cleveland, recently defending the institution of Masonry, declared that the *glory* of Masonry consists in its *exclusiveness*. But is this in accordance with the benevolence required in the Gospel?

Masonry, observe, professes to be a benevolent institution. But, first, it excludes all women from a participation in its rights, ceremonies, privileges, and blessings, whatever they may be. Secondly, it excludes all old men in their dotage. Thirdly, it excludes all young men in their nonage; that is, under twenty-one years of age. Several other classes are excluded; but these that I have named comprise a vast majority, probably not less than two-thirds of all mankind. Again, they admit no deformed person, and none but those who are physically perfect. In short, they admit none who are likely to become chargeable to the institution.

Some time since the Grand Lodge of the State of New York adopted a series of articles defining certain landmarks and principles of Freemasonry. These articles have been accepted and eulogized by the Masonic press The first is as follows. I quote it from the *American Freemason*, edited by "Robert Morris, Knight Templar, and author of various Masonic works," with his preface and strictures. These articles Mr. Morris regards as high Masonic authority. The number from which I quote is dated at Louisville, Kentucky, 8th of April, 5854, Masonic date, in other words, in 1854, fourteen years ago.

"Our New York brethren are eminent for the matchless ability with which their Grand Lodge documents are prepared. In this department they have set the example for others, and there are yet a few that would do well to look to the East for more light. We copy their 'Thirty-four Articles' with some condensation and a few comments of our own, and present them to our readers as a well-digested system of Masonic law and practice.

"'ARTICLE I. It is not proper to initiate into our lodges persons of the negro race; and their exclusion is in accordance with Masonic law, and the ancient charges and regulations Because of their depressed social condition; their general want of intelligence, which unfits them as a body to work in or adorn the craft; the impropriety of making them our equals in one place, when from their social condition and the circumstances which almost everywhere attach to them, we can not do so in others; their not being, as a general thing. *free-born;* the impossibility, or at least the difficulty, of ascertaining, if we once commence, their free birth, and where the line of intelligence and social elevation commences and ends, or divides portions of their race; and finally, their not being as a race "persons of good report," or who can be "well recommended" as subjects for initiation, their very seldom being persons who have any "trade, estate, office, occupation or visible way of acquiring an honest livelihood and working in the craft, as becomes members of this ancient and most honorable fraternity, who ought not only to earn what is sufficient for themselves and families, but likewise something to spare for works of charity and for supporting the ancient grandeur and dignity of the royal craft, eating no man's bread for naught;" and their general positive deficiency of natural endowments. All which would render it impossible, as a general thing, to conciliate and continue between them and us good will and private affection or brotherly love, which cements into one united body the members of this ancient fraternity.'

"COMMENT. These arguments can not be successfully controverted. We, in the Southern or slave-holding States, whose experience with the colored race is greater than that of others, affirm the New York doctrine in every particular. However occasional instances may be offered to the contrary, they are but the exceptions to prove the general rule, that the race ought not to amalgamate socially or physically.

"'ARTICLE II. No person of the negro race shall be examined or admitted as a visitor of any lodge of Masons under this jurisdiction, if made in an African lodge in North America. Because all such lodges are clandestine and without legal authority.'"

Here we have their benevolence unmasked. A *depressed social condition* is a bar to admission to this *benevolent society*. What if the Christian church should adopt such an article? Is this Christian benevolence? Is it consistent with Christian morality? *Christian ministers*, is this the morality you teach and practice? You profess to teach and practice the precepts of Christ, and join and hold fast to a society whose *law is* to exclude men for being in a *depressed social position*, whatever their *wants*, their *moral and religious character may be*. You boast of your benevolence and exclude the very class who have most need of sympathy and benevolence, and are *you a professed disciple, and perhaps a professed minister of Jesus.* SHAME!

But is this real benevolence, or Gospel morality? No, indeed! It is the very opposite of Gospel morality or true benevolence. In a recent number of the *National Freemason*—I think its date is the 18th of January—it is admitted by the editor of that great national organ that benevolent institutions have been so much multiplied that there is now seldom any call upon Masons for charitable donations. Yes, but who has multiplied these benevolent societies? Surely *Masons* have not done this. *Christians* have done it. And Masonry now seems forced to admit that Christian benevolence has covered the whole field, and left them nothing to do. So far as I have had experience in Freemasonry, I can say that I do not recollect a single instance in which the lodge to which I belonged ever gave any money to any charitable object whatever.

As a Freemason, I never was called upon, and to my recollection I never gave a cent as a Freemason, either to an individual as a matter of charity or to any object whatever. My dues and fees to the lodges, of course, I paid regularly; but that the money thus collected was given to any charitable object whatever I do not believe.

Again, Freemasonry, at the best, is but a *mutual insurance company*. Their oaths pledge them to assist each other, if in distress or in necessitous circumstances; and each other' families, if left in want. This they can well afford to do, on the principle of mutual insurance: for they have vast sums, almost incalculable in amount, taking the whole fraternity together; and they can lay out almost any amount of money in fitting up their sumptuous lodges of the higher degrees, in building Masonic temples, in seeking each other's promotion to office, and in defending each other in case any one of them commits a crime and is liable to suffer for it.

The following estimate, taken from a note in the revised edition of Bernard's "Light on Masonry," p. 96, will give some idea how large are the sums held by Masons. "Supposing that in the United States there are 500,000 Entered Apprentices, 400,000 Masters, and 200,000 Royal Arch Masons, also 10,000 Knights, and that they all paid the usual fees for the degrees, the amount would be the enormous sum of $11,250,000; the yearly interest of which, at seven per cent, is $787,500, which sum (allowing $100 to each individual) would support 7,875 persons.

Now, I ask: Do Masons, by their charities, support this number of poor in the United States? Do they support one-tenth part of this number? Supposing they do, is it necessary to give $10, or $50 for the privilege of contributing $1, $5, or $50 masonically? Must the privilege of being a charitable man be bought with gold? How many there are who have rendered themselves incompent to bestow charities, by their payment for and attendance on Masonic secrets and ceremonies! If all the money paid for the degrees of Masonry was applied to charitable purposes, the subject would appear differently; but it is principally devoted to the erection of Masonic temples, support of the Grand Lodges, and for *refreshment* for the craft, and I think I may add, for their support in *kidnapping and murder."*

It is no doubt true that but a very small part of their funds is ever used for the support of even their own poor. If it is, it behooves them to show it, and let the public know. They boast much of their benevolence; and the charities of Freemasons are frequently compared with those of the church—and that, too, boastfully; they maintaining that they are more benevolent and charitable, and do more for the poor and destitute than even the church has done.

But let us look at this. Is there any truth in all this boasting? What has Freemasonry done for *general education* in any part of the world? Let them tell us. Again, what has Freemasonry done for the general poor? Nothing. What have they done for their own poor, *as a matter of charity and benevolence?* Absolutely nothing. They have not even disbursed the funds which have been paid in for that purpose. Let them show, if they can, that on the principle of a mutual insurance society they have faithfully paid out *to their own poor* that fund which has been paid in by Masons for the purpose of securing to themselves and families, in case they should be reduced to poverty, what would meet their absolute necessities. We challenge them to show any such thing. We challenge them to show that, *on the principle of benevolence and charity,* they have really done anything for either the general poor or their own poor. *They* compare themselves with the Church of Christ in this respect! What have they done for the Southern poor during our great struggle, and during the long period of starvation and distress that has reigned in the South? What have Freemasons, as such, done for the freedmen? And what are they now doing? What have they done in any age of the world, as Freemasons, for Christian missions, for the conversion of the world, for the salvation of the souls of men? What! compare themselves boastfully with the Church of God, as being more benevolent than Christians?

The fact is, the Church of Christ has done ten thousand times as much for humanity as they have ever done. And she has not done it on the principle of a mutual insurance company, but as a matter of true benevolence, including in her charities the poor, the lowly, the halt and the blind, the old and the young, the black and the white.

The Church of Christ has done more for the *bodies* of men, ten thousand times more, than Freemasonry has ever done or ever will do.

Besides, the Church of Christ has poured out its treasure like a flood to enlighten mankind generally, to save their souls, and to do them good both for time and eternity. But what has Freemasonry done in this respect? Their boasted benevolence is a sham. I admit that they do sometimes afford relief to an indigent brother Mason, and to the families of such. I admit that they have often done this. But I maintain that this is not done as an act of *Christian* charity, but only as an act of *Ma-*

*sonic* charity; and that Masonic charity is only *the part payment of a debt.* Masons pay in their money to the Masonic fund; and this fund is that out of which their poor are helped, when they are helped at all.

What individuals do for individuals, on rare occasions, is but a trifle. Indeed, it is seldom that they are called on as individuals. The help granted to the poor is almost always taken from the funds of the lodges. And I seriously doubt whether there is a lodge in the United States that has ever paid as much for the support of their own poor as has been paid in to their funds by those who have joined the lodge. Let it be understood, then, that their boast of benevolence and of Christian morality is utterly false. Their oaths do not pledge them at all to the performance of any truly Christian morality; but to a Masonic benevolence, which is the opposite of true Christian morality.

Instead, therefore, of Masonry's inculcating really sound morality, instead of its being almost or quite true religion, the very perfection of that morality which their oaths oblige them to practice is anti-Christian, and opposed to both the law and gospel of God. It is partial. And here let me again appeal to the dear young men who have been persuaded to join the Masonic fraternity under the impression that it is a benevolent institution. Do not, my dear young men, suffer yourselves to be deceived in this respect. If you have well considered what the law and Gospel require, you will soon perceive that the benevolence and morality required by your Masonic oaths is not *Gospel* morality or *true* benevolence at all; but that it is altogether a *spurious* and *selfish* morality. Indeed, you yourselves are aware that you joined the lodge from selfish motives; and that the morality inculcated by Masons is an exclusive, one-sided, and selfish affair altogether. In some of the lectures, you are aware that occasionally the duty of universal good-will is, in few words, inculcated. But you also know that your oaths, which lay down the rule of your duty in this respect, require no such thing as universal and impartial benevolence; but that they require the *opposite* of this. That is, they require you to prefer a Mason because he is a Mason to a Christian because he is a Christian; and, instead of requiring you to do good especially to the household of faith, your oaths require you to do good especially to those who are Freemasons, whether they belong to the household of faith or not But this you know to be anti-Christian, and not according to the Gospel. But you know alas that Christians devote themselves to doing good to Masons and to those who are not Masons, to all classes and descriptions of men. And this they do, not on the principle, as I have said, of a mutual insurance society, but as a mere matter of benevolence. They deny themselves for the sake of doing good to the most lowly and even to the most wicked men.

Do not allow yourselves, therefore, to suppose that there is any *good* in Masonry. We often hear it said, and sometimes by professed Christians and Christian ministers, that "Masonry is a good thing."

But be not deceived. If by good is intended *morally* good, the assertion is false. *There is nothing morally good in Freemasonry.* If there are any good men who are Freemasons, Freemasonry has not made them so; but Christianity has made them so. They are good not by virtue of their Freemasonry, but by virtue of their Christianity. They have not been made good by anything they have found in Freemasonry; but, if they are good, they have been made good by Christianity, *in spite* of Freemasonry. I must say that I have always been ashamed of Freemasons whenever I have read, in their orations, or in the sermons of ministers who have eulogized it, or in their eulogistic books, the pretense that Freemasonry is a *benevolent* institution. Many have claimed it to be religion, and true religion. This question I shall examine in another place. But the thing I wish to fix your especial attention upon in the conclusion of this article is, that Freemasonry has no just claims to Christian morality or benevolence; but that in its best estate it is only partiality, and the doing in a very slovenly manner the work of a mutual insurance company. I do not claim that as a mutual insurance company it is necessarily wicked but I do insist that, being at best a mutual insurance company, it is wicked and shameful to flaunt their hypocritical professions of benevolence before the public as they constantly do. How long shall an intelligent people be nauseated with this pretense? How can they expect us to have the least respect for such claims to benevolence? We must regard the putting forth of such claims as an insult to our common sense.

## CHAPTER XV.

## FREEMASONRY IS A FALSE RELIGION

SOME Freemasons claim that Freemasonry is a saving institution, and that it is true religion. Others hold a different opinion, claiming that it is the *handmaid of religion*, a system of *refined morality*. Others still are free to admit that it is only a mutual aid or mutual insurance society. This discrepancy of views among them is very striking, as every one knows who has been in the habit of reading sermons, lectures, and orations on Masonry published by themselves. In this article I propose to inquire, first, Do their *standard authorities* claim that Masonry is identical with true religion? secondly, Does Freemasonry *itself* claim to be true religion? and, thirdly, Are these claims valid?

1. Do their standard authorities claim that Masonry is true religion?

I quote Salem Town. I read his work some forty years ago. The book professes on its title-page to be "A System of Speculative Masonry, exhibited in a course of lectures before the Grand Chapter of the State of New York, at their annual meetings in the City of Albany." It was reduced to a regular system by their special request, and recommended to the public by them as a system of Freemasonry. It is also recommended by nine grand officers, in whose presence the lectures were delivered; by another who had examined them; and by "the Hon. DeWitt Clinton, General Grand High Priest of the General Grand Chapter of the United States of America, Grand Master of the Grand Lodge of the State of New York, etc., etc."

The book was extensively patronized and subscribed for by Freemasons throughout the country, and has always been considered by the fraternity as a standard authority. From this author I quote as follows:

"The principles of Freemasonry have the same coeternal and unshaken foundations, contain and inculcate the same truths in substance, and propose the same ultimate end, as the doctrines of Christianity."—P. 53. Again he says: "The same system of faith and the same practical duties taught by revelation are contained in and required by the Masonic institution."—P. 174. "Speculative Masonry combines those great and fundamental principles which constitute the very essence of the

Christian system."—P. 37. "It is no secret that there is not a duty enjoined nor a virtue required in the volume of inspiration but what is found in and taught by Speculative Freemasonry." "The characteristic principles are such as embrace the whole subject-matter of divine economy."—P. 31.

Again he says: "As the WORD in the first verse of St. John constitutes both the foundation, the subject-matter, and the great ultimate end of the Christian economy, so does the same WORD, in all its relations to man, time, and eternity, constitute the very spirit and essence of Speculative Freemasonry."—P. 155. Again, referring to the promise of the Messiah, he says: "The same precious promise is the great corner-stone in the edifice of Speculative Freemasonry."—P. 171. Again he says: "The Jewish order of priesthood from Aaron to Zacharias, and even till the coming of Messias, was a confirmation of the great event, which issued in the redemption of man. All pointed to the eternal priesthood of the Son of God, who by his own blood made atonement for sin, and consecrated the way to the Holy of holies. *This constitutes the great and ultimate point of Masonic research.*"—P. 121

"That a knowledge of the divine WORD, or LOGOS, should have been the object of so much religious research from time immemorial adds not a little to the honor of Speculative Freemasonry."—P. 151.

Again he says: "It is a great truth, and weighty as eternity, that the present and ever lasting well-being of mankind is solely and ultimately intended."—P. 170. This he says of Freemasonry. But again he says: "Speculative Masonry, according to present acceptation, has an ultimate reference to that spritual building erected by virtue in the heart, and summarily implies the arrangement and perfection of those holy and sublime principles by which the soul is fitted for a meet temple of God in a world of immortality."—P. 63. Does not Freemasonry profess to be a saving *religion* ?

Again he says: "In advancing to the fourth degree, the good man is greatly encouraged to persevere in the ways of well-doing even to the end. He has a name which no man knoweth save him that receiveth it. If, therefore, he be rejected and cast forth among the rubbish of the world, he knows full well that the great Master-builder of the universe, having chosen and prepared him a lively stone in that spiritual building in the heavens, will bring him forth in triumph, while shouting grace, grace to the Divine Redeemer. Then the Freemason is assured of his election and *final salvation.* Hence, opens the fifth degree, where he discovers his election to, and his glorified station in, the kingdom of his Father." Then again he is assured of his "election and glorified station in the kingdom of his Father." If this is not claiming for Freemasonry a saving power what is? Salem Town is the great light in Freemasonry, as the title and history of his work imports. Does he not claim that Freemasonry is a saving *religion? To be sure he does,* or no words can assert such a claim. "With these views, the sixth degree is conferred, where the riches of divine grace are opened in boundless prospect." "Then he beholds in the eighth degree, that all the heavenly sojourners will be admitted within the veil of God's presence, where they will become kings and priests before the throne of his glory forever and ever."—Pp. 79-81. By the "heavenly sojourners," he certainly means Freemasons. Observe what he asserts of them: "Then he (the Freemason) beholds in the eighth degree that all the heavenly sojourners will be admitted within the veil of God's presence, where they will become kings and priests before *the throne of his glory forever and ever." This clenches the claim.* "The maxims of wisdom are gradually unfolded, till the whole duty of man is clearly and persuasively exhibited to the mind."—P. 184.

Again: "Principles and duties which lie at the foundation of the Masonic system, and are solemnly enjoined upon every brother; whoever, therefore, shall conscientiously discharge them in the fear of God fulfills the whole duty of man."—P. 48. Then he claims for Freemasonry all that is or can *be claimed for the law or Gospel of God.*

Again he says: "The Divine Being views no moral character in a man with greater complacency than his who in heart strictly conforms to Masonic requirements." "The more prominent features of a true Masonic character are literally marked with the highest beauties."—Pp. 33, 185. Then again he represents Masonry as forming as holy a character in man as the *Gospel does or can.*

Again he says that "every good Mason is of necessity truly and emphatically a Christian."—P. 37. Then he represents Freemasonry as indentical with Christianity. A true Mason must necessarily be a true Christian. That Masonry professes to conduct its disciples to heaven we find affirmed by Town, in the following language. Of the inducements to practice the precepts of Masonry he says: " They are found in that eternal weight of glory, that crown of joy and rejoicing laid up for the faithful in a future world."—P. 188.

By the faithful here he means faithful Freemasons. This same writer claims that Solomon organized the institution by inspiration from God. On page 187, he says: "So Masonry was transmitted from Enoch, through Noah, Abraham, Moses, and their successors, till Solomon, being inspired of God, established a regular form of administration."

This will suffice for the purpose of showing what is claimed for Masonry by their standard authorities. The same in substance might be quoted from various other standard writers. I have made these quotations from Elder Stearns' book, not finding in my library a copy of Town. In another place I shall find it convenient to quote sundry others of their standard writers, who, while they claim it to be a religion, do not consider it the Christian religion.

This conducts us (2) to the second inquiry: *What does Freemasonry claim for itself?*

And here I might quote from almost any of the Masonic degrees to show that this claim is put forth in almost every part of the whole institution. As Town claims for it, so it claims for itself, *a power to conduct its disciples to heaven.* Any one who will take pains to read

Bernard's "Light on Masonry" through, will be satisfied that Town claims for the institution no more than it claims for itself.

I beg of all who feel any interest in this subject to get and read Bernard on Masonry; to read it through, and see if Town has not rightly represented the claims of Freemasonry. I deny, observe, that he has rightly represented its *principles*, and that which it really *requires* of Masons. That he has *mis*represented *Masonic law* I insist. But in respect to its promises of heaven as a reward for being good Freemasons he has not misrepresented it. It claims to be a saving institution. This certainly will appear to any person who will take the pains to examine its teachings and its claims as revealed in "Light on Masonry." Mr. Town has grossly misrepresented Masonic *law* and *morality* as we have seen in examining its claims to benevolence, and in scrutinizing their oaths and their profane use of Scripture. But that Mr. Town has not misrepresented the *claims* of Masonry to be a saving religion has been abundantly shown in these pages by quotations from "Light on Masonry." I might quote many pages from the body of Masonry where it teaches the candidates that the observance of Masonic *law*, *principles* and *usages* will secure his salvation. The Gospel professes no more than this, that those who obey *it* shall be saved. Surely Masonry claims to be a saving religion just as much as the Gospel of Christ does.

Just take the following from the degree of "The Knights of the East and West." "Light on Masonry," first edition, p. 217, already quoted in another place.

In explaining the ceremony of sounding the seventh trumpet, and conducting the candidate to the vacant canopy, we find the following: "*This canopy it will be recollected is at the right side of the All Puissant who represents* JEHOVAH. *The sounding of the seventh trumpet, and the conducting of the candidate to the vacant canopy, is a representation of the end of the world, and the glorification of all true Masons at the right hand of God, having passed through the trials of Freemasonry and washed their robes in their own blood.*" If Freemasonry does not claim to be a saving religion how can such a claim be made? The compiler adds: "If this is not Antichrist what is?", But I must beg of the reader to examine the books that reveal Masonry for themselves, since to quote the claims of Masonry on this head further than I have done, would not only be useless and tiresome, but would swell this work too much.

This brings me (3) to the third inquiry: Are

the claims that Masonry is a true and saving religion valid?

To this question I reply that it is *utterly false;* and in this respect Freemasonry is a *fatal delusion.* From the quotations that I have made from Town, it will be perceived that he represents Freemasonry as identical with Christianity.

Mr. Preston is another of their standard writers. I quote the following note from Stearns on Masonry, p. 28: "Mr. Preston's book, entitled 'Illustrations of Masonry,' has been extensively patronized by the fraternity as a standard work. The copy before me is the first American, from the tenth London edition." Mr. Preston says in his book, p. 30: "The universal principles of the art unite in one indissoluble bond of affection men of the most opposite tenets, of the most distant countries, and of the most contradictory opinions." Again, p. 125, he says: "Our celebrated annotator has taken no notice of Masons having the art of working miracles, and foresaying things to come. But this was certainly not the least important of their doctrines. Hence, astrology was admitted as one of the arts which they taught, and the study of it warmly recommended."

"This study became, in the course of time,

a regular science." So here we learn that Masons formerly claimed the power of working miracles. I quote again from Bradley, p. 8. He says: "We leave every member to choose and support those principles of religion and those forms of government which appear consistent to his views." In the work of Preston, p. 51, we have the following: "As a Mason, you are to study the moral law as contained in the sacred code, the Bible; *and in countries where that book is not known, whatever is understood to contain the will or law of God.*" O, then, in every country Masons are to embrace the prevalent religion, *whatever it may be*, and accept whatever is claimed in any country where they may reside, *to be the law and will of God.* But is this Christianity, or consistent with it? It is well known and admitted that Masonry claims to have descended from the earliest ages, and that the institution has existed in all countries and under all religions; and that the ancient philosophers of Greece and Rome, the astrologers and soothsayers, and the great men of all heathen nations have belonged to that fraternity.

It is also well known that at this time there are multitudes of Jews, Mohammedans, and skeptics of every grade belonging to the institution. I do not know that this is denied by any intelligent Mason. Now, if this is so, how can Freemasonry be the true religion, or at all consistent with it? Multitudes of Universalists and Unitarians, and of errorists of every grade, are Freemasons; and yet Freemasonry itself claims to save its disciples, to conduct them to heaven!

The third question proposed for discussion in my last number is: *Are the claims of Masonry to be a true and saving institution valid?* To this I answer, No. This will appear if we consider, first, that *the morality which it inculcates is not the morality of the law and Gospel of God.* The law and the Gospel, as I have shown in a former number, lay down the same rule of life. And Christ, in commenting upon the true meaning and spirit of the law, says: "If ye love them that love you, what thank have ye? Do not even the publicans the same?" He requires us to love our enemies, and to pray for them, as truly as for our friends. In short, he requires *universal benevolence;* whereas Freemasonry requires no such thing. Its oaths, which are its law, simply require its members to be just to each other. I say just, for their boasted benevolence is simply the payment of a debt.

They do, indeed, promise to assist each other in distress, and to help each other's families, provided they fall into poverty. But on what condition do they promise this? Why, that a certain amount is to be paid into their treasury as a fund for this purpose. But this, surely, is not benevolence, but the simple payment of a debt, on the principle of mutual insurance.

This I have abundantly shown in a former number. Again, the *motives* presented in Freemasonry to secure the course of action to which they are pledged are by no means consistent with the law or the Gospel of God In religion, and in true morality, everything depends on the motive or reason for the performance of an action. God accepts nothing that does not proceed from supreme love to Him and equal love to our fellow-men. Not merely to our brother Masons; but to our neighbor—that is, to all mankind. Whatever does not proceed from love and faith is sin, according to the teachings of the Bible. And by love, I say again, is meant the supreme love of God and the equal love of our neighbor.

But Masonry teaches no such morality as this. The motive urged by Masons is, to honor Masonry, to honor the institution, to honor each other. While they are pledged to assist each other in distress; to keep each other's secrets, even if they be crimes; and to aid each other.

whether right or wrong. so far as to extricate them from any difficulty in which they are involved; yet they never present the pure motives of the Gospel. They are pledged not to violate the chastity of a brother Mason's wife, sister, daughter, or mother; but they are not pledged by Masonry, as the law and Gospel of God require, to abstain from such conduct with any female whatever. But nothing short of *universal* benevolence, and *universal* morality, is acceptable to God.

But again: It has been shown that Masonry claims to be a *saving institution;* that this is claimed for it by the highest Masonic authorities; and that this claim is one set up by itself as well. But an examination of Freemasonry shows that it promises salvation upon *entirely other conditions than those revealed in the Gospel of Christ.* The Gospel nowhere inculcates the idea that any one can be saved by obedience to the law of God. "By the deeds of the law shall no flesh be justified" is the uniform teaching of the Bible. Much less can any one be saved by conformity to *Masonic* law, which requires only a partial, and therefore a spurious, morality. The Bible teaches that all unconverted persons are in a state of sin, of total moral depravity, and consequent condemnation by the law of God: and that the conditions of salvation are *repentance* and a total renunciation of all sin, *faith in our Lord Jesus Christ*, and *sanctification* by the *Holy Spirit*. Now these are by no means the conditions upon which Freemasonry proposes to save its members. The teachings of Freemasonry upon this subject are summarily this: *Obey Masonic law, and live.*

Now, surely, whatever promises heaven to men upon other conditions than those proposed in the Gospel of Christ is a *fatal delusion* And this Freemasons can not deny, for they profess to accept the Bible as true. Freemasonry lays no stress at all upon conversion to Christ by the Holy Spirit. It presents no means or motives to secure that result. The idea of being turned from sin to holiness, from a self-pleasing spirit to a supreme love of God, by the preaching of the Gospel, accompanied by the Holy Spirit, is not taught in Freemasonry.

It nowhere recognizes men as being justified by faith in Christ, as being sanctified by faith in Christ, and as being saved as the Gospel recognizes men as being saved.

Indeed, it is salvation by Masonry, and not salvation by the Gospel, that Masonry insists upon. It is another gospel, or presents entirely another method of salvation than that presented in the Gospel. How can it be pretended by those who admit that the Gospel is true that men can be saved by Freemasonry at all? If Freemasons are good men, it is not Freemasonry that has made them so; but the Gospel has made them so, *in spite* of Freemasonry. If they are anything more than self-righteous, it is because of the teachings of the Gospel; for certainly Freemasonry teaches a very different way of salvation from that which the Gospel reveals. But, again, the prayers recorded in Freemasonry, and used by them in their lodges, are not Christian prayers; that is, they are not prayers offered in the name of Christ.

But the Gospel teaches us that it is fundamental to acceptable prayer that it be offered in the name of Christ. Again, as we have seen in a former number, the teachings of Freemasonry are *scandalously false;* and their ceremonies are a mockery, and truly shocking to Christian feelings.

Again, Freemasonry is a system of gross hypocrisy. It professes to be a saving institution, and promises salvation to those who keep its oaths and conform to its ancient usages. It also professes to be entirely consistent with the Christian religion. And this it does while it embraces as good and acceptable

Masons hundreds of thousands who abhor Christianity, and scoff at the Bible and everything that the Bible regards as sacred. In a Christian nation it professes to receive Christianity as a true religion; in Mohammedan countries it receives the Koran as teaching the true religion; in heathen countries it receives their sacred books as of as much authority as that which is claimed in Christian countries for the Bible. In short, Freemasonry in a pagan country is pagan, in a Mohammedan country it is Mohammedan, and in a Christian country it professes to be Christian; but in this profession it is not only grossly inconsistent, but intensely hypocritical.

Notwithstanding all the boasts that are made in its lower degrees of its being a true religion, if you will examine the matter through to the end, you will find that, as you ascend in the scale of degrees, the mask is gradually thrown off, until we come to the "Philosophical Lodge," in the degree of the "Knights Adepts of the Eagle or Sun;" in which, as will be seen, no concealment is longer attempted. I will make a short quotation from this degree, as any one may find it in "Light on Masonry."—

"*Requisitions to make a good Mason.*—If you ask me what are the requisite qualities that a Mason must be possessed of to come to the center of truth, I answer you that you must crush the head of the serpent, ignorance You must shake off the yoke of infant prejudice, concerning the mysteries of the reigning religion, which worship has been imaginary and only founded on the spirit of pride, which envies to command and be distinguished, and to be at the head of the vulgar in affecting an exterior purity, which characterizes a false piety joined to a desire of acquiring that which is not its own, and is always the subject of this exterior pride and unalterable source of many disorders; which, being joined to gluttonness, is the daughter of hypocrisy, and employs every matter to satisfy carnal desires, and raises to these predominant passions altars upon which she maintains without ceasing the light of iniquity, and sacrifices continually offerings to luxury, voluptuousness, hatred, envy, and perjury.

"Behold, my dear brother, what you must fight against and destroy before you can come to the knowledge of the true good and sovereign happiness! Behold this monster which you must conquer—a serpent which we detest as an idol that is adored by the idiot and vulgar under the name of religion!"—See 'Light on Masonry," pp. 270, 271. 8th edition.

Here, then, Masonry stands revealed, after all its previous pretensions to being a true religion, as the unalterable opponent of the reigning or Christian religion. That it claims to be a religion is indisputable; but that it is not the Christian religion is equally evident. Nay, it finally comes out flat-footed, and represents the reigning or Christian religion as a serpent which Masons detest, as an idol which is adored by the idiot and vulgar under the name of religion.

Now let professed Christians who are Freemasons examine this for themselves. Do not turn away from examination of this subject.

And here, before I close this article, I beg to be understood that I have no quarrel with individual Masons. It is with the system that I have to deal. The great mass of the fraternity are utterly deceived, as I was myself. Very few, comparatively, of the fraternity are at all acquainted with what is really taught in the higher degrees as they ascend from one to another. None of them know anything of these degrees any further than they have taken them, unless they have studied them in the books as they are revealed. I can not believe that Christian men will remain connected with this institution, if they will only examine it for themselves and look it through to the end. I know that young Masons, and those who have only taken the lower degrees, will be shocked at what I have just quoted from a higher degree. I was so myself when first I examined the higher degrees. But you will inquire how, and in what sense, are we who have only taken the lower degrees responsible for the oaths and teachings of the higher degrees, which we have not taken. In a future number I shall briefly answer this question. Most Freemasoms, and many who have been Masters of lodges of the lower degrees, are really so ignorant of what Masonry as a whole is, that when they are told the simple truth respecting it, they really believe that what you tell them is a lie. I am receiving letters from this class of Freemasons, accusing me of lying and misrepresentation, which accusations I charitably ascribe to ignorance. To such I say, Wait, gentlemen, until you are better informed upon the subject, and you will hold a different opinion.

I have quoted from Salem Town showing that he claims that Solomon established the institution by divine authority—that Town claims for it all that is claimed for Christianity as a saving religion. I might show that others of their standard writers set up the same claim. Now I am unwilling to believe that these writers are hypocrites. It must be that they have been imposed upon as I was. They were ignorant of the origin of Freemasonry. Perhaps this was not strange, especially as regards Mr. Town; for until within the last half century this matter has not been searched to the bottom. But certainly there is now no excuse for the ignorant or dishonest assertions that are so often made by Freemasons. Such pretenses palmed off, as they now often are, upon those whose occupation or other causes forbid their examination of the subject, ought to arouse the righteous indignation of every honest citizen. I say it *ought* to do so; yes, and it *must* do so, when we see our dear young men lured by false pretenses in crowds into this snare of Satan. They get drawn in and *committed*, and, as we see, are afraid to be convinced of their error and become uncandid and will not honestly examine the subject. They will shun the light when it is offered. Can men be saved in this state of mind?

## CHAPTER XVI.

### THE ARGUMENT THAT GREAT AND GOOD MEN HAVE BEEN AND ARE FREEMASONS, EXAMINED.

IT is the universal practice of Freemasons to claim as belonging to their fraternity a great many wise and good men.

As I have shown in a former number, Masonry itself claims to have been founded by Solomon, and to have been patronized by St. John. Their lodges are dedicated to St. John and Zerubbabel, as I have shown; and Solomon figures more or less prominently in a great number of their degrees. Now it has already been shown by their highest authorities that this claim of having been founded by Solomon and patronized by St. John is utterly without foundation. Strange to tell, while it claims to have always been one and identical, and that it never has been changed, still on the very face of the different degrees it is shown that the great majority of them are of recent origin. If, as their best historians assert, Speculative

Freemasonry dates no further back than the eighteenth century, of course, the claim of Freemasons that their institution was established and patronized by inspired men can command no respect or confidence.

But, if this claim is false, what reason have we to have confidence in their assertions that so many great and good men of *modern* times were Freemasons. Investigation will prove that this claim is to a very great extent without foundation. It has been asserted here with the utmost confidence, over and over again, that Bishop McIlvaine was a Freemason. But having recently been written to on the subject, he replied that he never was a Freemason.

Again, it is no doubt true that many men have joined them, and, when they have taken a sufficient number of degrees to have the impression entirely removed from their minds that there is any secret in Freemasonry worth knowing, they have become disgusted with its shams, its hypocrisies, its falsehoods, its oaths and its ceremonies, its puerilities and its blasphemies; and they have paid no further attention to it.

Freemasons have paraded the fact that Gen. Washington was a Mason before the public. The following conclusion of a letter from him will speak for him, and show how little he had to do with Masonry. Before his death he warned the whole country to beware of secret societies. The letter alluded to is dated "Mt. Vernon, September 25, 1798." Here we have its conclusion. It needs no comment:

"I have little more to add than thanks for your wishes, and favorable sentiments, except to correct an error you have run into of my presiding over the English lodges in this country. The fact is I preside over none, nor have I been in one more than once or twice within the last thirty years. I believe, notwithstanding, that none of the lodges in this country are contaminated with the principles ascribed to the society of the Illuminati.

"Signed, GEORGE WASHINGTON."

I might quote numerous instances in which good men have at first hesitated, and finally refused to go any further in Masonry, and have threatened to expose the whole of it to the world. Whoever will read Elder Stearns' little books on Masonry will find examples of this.

But why should Freemasons lay so much *stress* on the fact that many good men have been Freemasons? It has always been the favorite method of supporting a bad institution to claim as its patrons the wise and good.

This argument might have been used with great force, and doubtless was, in favor of *idolatry* in the time of Solomon and the prophets. Several of the kings of Israel were idolaters, as well as the queens and the royal family generally.

The great mass of the prophets, and religious teachers, and great men of the nation, lapsed into idolatry. Nearly all the learning, and wealth and influence of the whole nation could be appealed to as rejecting Christ. Those who received him were but a few fishermen, with some of the lowest of the people. Now what a powerful argument was this! If the argument of Masons be of any value, how overwhelming an argument must this have been against the claims of our Lord Jesus Christ!

Why the rejecters of Jesus could quote all the *great* men of the nation, and the *pious* men, and the *wise* men, as decidedly opposed to his claims! The same was true after his death and resurrection for a great while. The question would often arise: "Do any of the *rulers* believe on him?"

An institution is not to be judged by the conduct of a few of its members who might have been either worse or better than its principles. Christianity, *e. g.*, is not to be judged by the conduct of particular professed Christians; but by its laws, its principles, by what it justifies and by what it condemns. Christianity condemns all iniquity. It abhors *covering up iniquity*. In the case of its greatest and most prominent professors, it exposes and denounces their sin, and never justifies it. But Masonry, on the other hand, is a secret work of darkness. It requires its members to take an oath to cover up each other's sins. It requires them to swear, under the most awful penalties, that they will seek the condign punishment of every one who in any instance violates any point of their obligation. It, therefore, justifies the murder of those who betray its secrets.

Masons consistently justified the murder of Morgan, as everybody in this country knows who has paid any attention to the subject.

This is not inconsistent with their principles. Indeed, it is the very thing demanded, the very thing promised under oath.

But again: This same argument, by which Masons are attempting to sustain their institution, was always resorted to to sustain the practice of slaveholding.

Why, how many wise and good men, it was said, were slaveholders. The churches and ecclesiastical bodies at the North were full of charity in respect to them. They could not denounce slaveholding as a sin.

They would say that it was an *evil;* but for a long time they could not be persuaded to pronounce it a *moral* evil, a sin. And why? Why, because so many doctors of divinity were slaveholders and were defending the institution. Because a large portion of the church, of nearly every denomination, were involved in the abomination. "They are *good men*," it was said; "they are *great* men—we must be charitable."

And so, when this horrid civil war came on, these great and good men, that had sustained the institution of slavery, sustained and stimulated the war.

Many of them took up arms, and fought with desperation to sustain the institution. But what is thought now—at least throughout all the North, and throughout all the Christian world—of the *great* and *good* men who have done this thing? Who does not now admit that they were deluded? that they had anything but the Spirit of Christ? that they were in the hands of the Devil all along?

The fact is, this has always been the device of those who have sustained any system of wickedness. They have taken pains, in one way and another, to draw into their ranks men of reputation for wisdom and piety, men of high standing in Church and State. A great many of those who are claimed by Freemasons to be of their number never were Freemasons at all. Others were entrapped into it, and turned a "cold shoulder" upon it, and paid no more attention to it; but were ever after claimed as Freemasons.

But there are great multitudes of Freemasons who have taken some of the degrees, and have become heartily disgusted with it. But, knowing that Freemasons are under oath to persecute and even murder them if they publicly renounce it and expose its secrets, they remain quiet, say nothing about it, and go no further with it; but are still *claimed* as Freemasons. As soon as public sentiment is enough aroused to make them feel safe in doing what they regard as their solemn duty, great numbers of them will no doubt publicly renounce it. At present they are afraid to do so. They are afraid that their business will be ruined, their characters assailed, and their lives at least put in jeopardy.

But it should be understood that, while it may be true that there are many pious and wise men belonging to the Masonic fraternity, yet there are thousands of learned and pious men who have renounced it, and thousands more who have examined its claims, and who reject it as an imposture and as inconsistent either with Christianity or good government.

It is sometimes said: "Those men that renounced Masonry in the days of Morgan are dead. There are now thousands of *living* witnesses. Why should we take the testimony of the dead instead of that of the living? The living we know; the dead we do not know."

To this I answer, first: There are thousands of renouncing Masons still living who reiterate their testimony on all proper occasions against the institution. Many of them we know, or *may* know; and *they* are not dead witnesses, but living. Now, if it was wickedness that led those men to renounce Freemasonry and publish its secrets, how is it that no instance has ever occurred in which a seceding Freemason has renounced and denounced his renunciation, and gone back into the ranks of Freemasons? I have never heard of such a case. It is well for the cause of truth that this question has come up again before the Masons that renounced the institution in the days of Morgan *were* all dead. It is well that hundreds and thousands of them are still alive, and are still living witnesses, bearing their steady and unflinching testimony against the institution.

But, again: The present living witnesses

who testify in its behalf, let it be remembered, are *interested* witnesses. They still adhere to the institution. They are under oath not to speak against it, but in every way to support it. Of what value, then, is their testimony in its favor?

The fact is, we have their secrets published; and these books speak for themselves. Let the living or the dead say what they may, the truth is established that these books truly reveal Masonry; and by this revelation let the institution stand or fall.

If any thing can be established by human testimony, it is established that Bernard's "Light on Masonry" has revealed Masonry substantially as it is. Bernard is still living. He is an old man; but he has recently said: "What I have written I have written on this subject. I have nothing to add, and I have nothing to retract." And there are still hundreds and thousands of men who know that he has published the truth. How vain and frivolous, then, is the inquiry, "Why should we not take the testimony of living rather than of dead witnesses?" The prophets and apostles are dead. Why not take the testimony of living skeptics that we know? Some of them are learned and respectable men. Alas! if dead men are not to be believed!

## CHAPTER XVII.

## MASONIC OATHS ARE UNLAWFUL AND VOID.

BECAUSE, 1st, they are *forbidden* by *Christ.* Matt. v 34–37. Whatever may be said of oaths administered by magistrates for governmental purposes, it can not be reasonably doubted that this teaching prohibits the taking of extrajudicial oaths. But Masonic oaths are extrajudicial.

2. Because they are awfully profane. "Thou shalt not take the name of the Lord thy God in vain." Exod. xx. 7. Certainly both the administering and taking of these oaths are taking the name of God in vain.

3. Because they swear to do unlawful things.

1. We have seen that all Masons swear to conceal all the secrets of Masonry that may be communicated to them. This is rash, and contrary to Lev. v. 4, 5: "*Or if a soul swear pronouncing with his lips to do evil, or to do good, whatsoever it be that a man shall pro-*

*nounce with an oath, and it be hid from him; when he knoweth of it, then he shall be guilty in one of these. And it shall be, when he shall be guilty in one of these things, that he shall confess that he hath sinned in that thing."* THE SIN MUST BE CONFESSED.

2. They swear to conceal each other's crimes. This we have seen. This is a conspiracy against all good government in Church and State. Is not this *wicked?*

3. They swear to deliver a brother Royal Arch Mason out of any difficulty and to espouse his cause so far as to extricate him from the same, if in their power, whether he be right or wrong. Is not this wicked? How this oath must lead to the defeat of the execution of law. It has defeated the ends of justice often, as every intelligent Mason may and ought to know.

4. They swear to give political preferment to a Mason, because he is a Mason, over one of equal qualifications, who is not a Mason. This is swearing to be partial. But is it not wicked to be partial? Can an oath to be partial make partiality a virtue? By swearing to do wrong can a man make it his duty, and, therefore, right to do wrong? *No indeed.*

5. They swear to persecute all who violate Masonic oaths as long as they live—to ruin

their reputation, derange their business, and, if they go from place to place, to follow them with representations of being worthless vagabonds. Is not this a promise under oath to do wickedly? Suppose those who violate Masonic oaths are enemies of Masonry, as well they may be, and as they ought to be, is it right to seek, in any way, to ruin them? Is this loving an enemy? Is not such persecution forbidden by every precept of both law and Gospel? Hence the declaration by the pen of inspiration: "Recompense to no man evil for evil. * * If thine enemy hunger, feed him; if he thirst, give him drink; for in so doing thou shalt heap coals of fire on his head." —Rom. xii. 17-20. And it is in direct opposition to the requirement. Matt. v. 44: "But I say unto you, Love your enemies, bless them that curse you, do good to them that hate you, and pray for them which despitefully use you, and persecute you."

6. They swear to seek the death or condign punishment of all who violate Masonic oaths. This we have seen! But is not this abominable wickedness? Is it not murder in intention, and, therefore, really murder, whether they succeed or not? To be sure it is.

7. They swear to seek revenge and to take vengeance on those who violate Masonic oaths

and to avenge the treason, as they call it, by the death of the traitor. This, also, we have seen. Now, is not this the perfection of wickedness? Ought not Masons to be put under bonds to keep the peace?

8. They swear to support Freemasonry, an institution, as we have seen, that ought not to exist in any community. These are only some of the reasons for pronouncing the oaths of Freemasonry utterly unlawful.

### MASONIC OATHS ARE NULL AND VOID.

1. Because they are obtained by fraud. The candidate for the first degree is assured by the master, in the most solemn manner, when the candidate is on his knees and about to take the oath, there is nothing in it inconsistent with his duty either to God or to man. But he finds, after taking and reflecting upon it, that he has made promises inconsistent with his duty both to God and man. This, of itself, makes the oath null.

2. They are void because they pledge the candidate to sin against God and man. 1st. By swearing to commit a sin, a man can not make it his *duty*, and, therefore, *right* to do *wrong*. He can not make *sin holiness*, or *crime* a *virtue*, by taking an oath to do it. Forty men took an oath that they would

neither eat nor drink until they had killed Paul. Were they under moral obligation, therefore, to kill him? If they were, it was their *duty*. If it was their *duty*, their killing him would have been a *holy* act. Who does not see the absurdity of this? To keep a wicked promise or oath is only adding sin to sin. But it maybe said that we are required to perform our vows. Yes, when we vow to do what is right, but not when we vow to do what is wrong. This is not only the doctrine of the Bible, but, also, of all the able writers on moral philosophy. It is, indeed, a self-evident truth. An oath to do wrong is sin. To perform it is adding sin to sin. All oaths to do wrong, or to refrain from doing right, are *null.*

### ALL FREEMASONS OUGHT TO RENOUNCE THEIR MASONIC OATHS.

1. Because they are profane and wicked.
2. Because they ought to repent the taking of them.
3. But repentance consists in heart-renunciation of them. A man can not repent of, without forsaking them.
4. If not repented of and forsaken, *i. e.*, renounced, the sin can not be forgiven.
5. Heart-renunciation must produce life-renunciation of them.

6. A sin is not repented of while it is concealed and not confessed to those who have been injured by it.

7. A sin against society or against individuals can not be forgiven, when just confession and restitution are withheld.

8. Masonic oaths are a conspiracy against God and man, and are not repented of while adhered to.

9. They are adhered to, while heart-renunciation is withheld.

10. Refusing to renounce is adherence.

11. Adherence makes them partakers of the crimes of Freemasons—" partakers of other men's sins." Because, to adhere is to justify their oaths and the keeping and fulfillment of them. But to justify their crimes, the murder of Morgan for example, is to partake of the guilt of his murderers.

12. While a Mason adheres his word can not be credited on questions relating to the secrets of Masonry.

13. Nor can his testimony be believed against one who has violated Masonic oaths, because he is sworn to ruin his reputation, and to represent him as a worthless vagabond.

14. An adhering Mason is a dangerous man in society. If he does as he is sworn to do,

is he not a dangerous man? If he does not do what he is sworn to do, and yet does not renounce his oath, he is a dangerous man, because he violates an oath, the obligation of which he acknowledges. Is not he a dangerous man who disregards the solemnity of an oath? But, perhaps, he is convinced that he ought not to do what he has sworn to do, and, therefore, does not do it, but still he adheres in the sense that he will not confess and renounce the sinfulness of the obligation. Is not that a dangerous man who sees the wrong of an oath and will not renounce it.

15. While he adheres to his Masonic oaths, he ought not to be trusted with the office of a magistrate. How should he, if he means to perform his Masonic vows?

16. Nor, while he adheres, should he be trusted with the office of sheriff, marshal, or constable. If he intends to perform his Masonic vows, it is madness to trust him with an office in Church or State.

17. If and while he adheres, he ought not to be received as a witness or juror when a Freemason is a party. This has been ruled as law.

18. Nor should he have power to appoint officers, as he will surely unduly favor Masons.

19. Nor should he have the control of funds and the bestowment of governmental patron-

age. This he will certainly abuse, if he keeps and performs his vows.

20. Nor should he be intrusted with the pardoning power. I wish it could be known in how many instances Freemasons have been pardoned and turned loose upon the public by governors and presidents who were Freemasons, and who were sworn to deliver them from any difficulty, whether right or wrong.

21. Nor should he be a post-master, as he will surely abuse his office to favor Masonry, and to persecute anti-Masons, if he keeps his vows. Of this we are having abundant proof.

22. While he adheres, his testimony against renouncing Masons ought not to be credited, because he has sworn to ruin their reputation and their business, and, until their death, to represent them to others as worthless vagabonds. Is a man's testimony against another worthy of credit, when he is thus sworn to hold him up to the world? We have no right to receive such testimony. It is the greatest injustice to credit the testimony of one who has taken and adheres to this oath, if he testifies against a renouncing Mason.

23. Those Masons who have taken and adhere to the vow to thus persecute, and the vow to avenge the treason of violating Masonic oaths by the death of the traitor, should

be held to bail to keep the peace. If they intend to perform their vows, they are eminently dangerous persons, and should be imprisoned or held to bail. Let no one say that this is harsh. Indeed, it is not. It is only common sense and common justice. Only remember what they are sworn to do, and that they *intend* to perform their vows, and then tell me is it safe and just that such men should be at large, and not even be put under bonds not to fulfill their vows. We must take the ground, either that they will not fulfill their vows, or we must hold that they ought not to be at large without adequate bail. I am aware that some will say that this is a harsh and extreme conclusion. But pray let me ask do you not feel and say this because you do not believe that there is *real danger* of Freemasons doing what they have sworn to do? If they have sworn as Bernard and others represent, and if they really intend to fulfill their vows, and if you admit this, is my conclusion harsh and extreme? When no occasion arises, calling for the fulfillment of their horrid oaths, they appear to be harmless and even good citizens. But let any man read the history of the abduction and murder of Morgan, as found in "Light on Masonry," and see how many men were engaged in it. Let him understand now this horrid murder was justified by the Grand Lodge, and by many *respectable citizens*. Let him ponder the fact that the men engaged in that affair were accounted respectable and good citizens; that a number of them were men high in office and in public confidence, and that the conspiracy extended over a wide territory, and then let him say whether, if an occasion arise demanding their action, they will prove to be law-abiding citizens, or, if they will not, as they have often done before, set at naught any law of God and man, and, if need be, reach their end through the blood of their victim.

But some will say that this is representing Freemasonry as *infamous*, and holding it up to the *disgust, contempt,* and *indignation* of mankind. I reply, I have not misrepresented it, as it is revealed in the books which I have been examining. Remember, it is with Masonry as *there revealed* that I have to deal. If a truthful representation of it excites the *contempt, disgust,* and *indignation* of the public toward it—if to rightly represent Freemasonry is to render it *infamous*, I can not help it. The fault, if any, is not mine. I have revealed nothing. I have only called attention to facts of common concern to all honest citizens. Let the infamy rest where it belongs.

## CHAPTER XVIII.

### WHY FREEMASONS RESORT TO THREATS AND REFUSE TO DISCUSS THEIR PRINCIPLES.

THERE are many aspects of this subject that need to be thoroughly considered by all men. For example, the bearing of this institution upon domestic happiness is of great importance.

The stringent secrecy enjoined and maintained at the hazard of one's life, is really inconsistent with the spirit of the marriage contract. It is really an insult to a wife for a husband to go and pledge himself to conceal from his wife that which he freely communicates to strangers. Suppose that wives should get up lodges, spend their money and their time in secret conclave, absent themselves from home, and swear to keep their proceedings entirely from their husbands; and suppose that such organizations should be made permanent, and extend throughout the length and breadth of the land, would husbands endure this ! Would they think it right ?

In short, if wives should do what husbands do, would not husbands rebel, think themselves abused, and insist upon such a course being entirely and forever abandoned? Indeed they would! How can a man look his wife in the face after joining a Masonic lodge? I have recently received several letters from the wives of Masons complaining of this:—that their husbands had joined the lodge and paid their money, and were spending their time, and concealing their doings and their principles from their wives. This is utterly unjust. It is shameful; and no honorable man can reflect upon it without feeling that he wrongs his wife.

Of late, partly to appease women, and partly to give the female relatives of Masons certain signs and tokens by which they may make themselves known as the wives or daughters, sisters or mothers, of Freemasons, they are conferring certain side degrees upon women. Of this Freemasons themselves—that is the more honorable among them—are complaining as an innovation, and as a thing justly to be complained of by outsiders. And observe that they ask, what if these daughters or sisters of Masons, who are taking these side degrees, should marry men who are not Masons, and who are opposed to the institution,—what would be the consequence of this? You administer, they say, the degrees for the sake of preserving domestic peace; and here, on the other hand, it would produce domestic discord.

But again, it should be considered that Masonry is an institution of vast proportions, and of such a nature that it will not allow its principles to be discussed.

It works in the dark. And instead of standing or falling according to its character and tendencies, when brought to the light, when thoroughly discussed and understood by the public, it closes the door against all discussion, shrouds itself in midnight, and its argument is assassination. Now, what have we here in a republican government? A set of men under oath to assist each other, and even to conceal each other's crimes, embracing and acting upon principles that are not to be discussed!

Immediately after the publication of the first number of my articles in the *Independent*, on the subject of Masonry, I received a threatening letter from the city of New York, virtually threatening me with assassination. I have since received several letters of the most abusive character from Freemasons, simply because I discuss and expose their principles. Now, if their principles can not bear the light, they never should be tolerated. It is an insult to any community for a set of men to band themselves together to keep each other's secrets, and to aid each other in a great variety of ways, and refuse to have their principles known and discussed, whilst their only argument is a dagger, a bullet, and a bowie knife, instead of truth and reason. Indeed, it is well-known throughout the length and breadth of the land that Masonry is so determined not to have its principles discussed, that men are afraid to discuss them. They expect from the very nature of Masonry, and from the revelations that it has made of itself, to be persecuted, and perhaps murdered, if they attempt to discuss the principles and usages of that institution. Now, is such a thing as this to be tolerated in a free government? Why how infinitely dangerous and shocking is this!

Everything else may be discussed. All governmental proceedings, the characters of public men, all institutions of learning, all benevolent societies, and indeed everything else in the world may be discussed, and criticised, and held up for public examination; but Masonry, forsooth, must not be touched. It must work in the dark. All the moneys received by charitable institutions must be reported; and the manner in which they dispose of every dollar that they receive must be held up before the public for examination. Every one sees the importance of this, and knows that it is right. But Freemasonry will make no report of its funds. They will not tell us what they do with them. They will not allow themselves to be called in question. No, that institution must not be ventilated upon pain of persecution unto death.

Now, it is enough to make a man's blood boil with indignation that such an institution as this should exist in the land. And what is most astonishing is, that members of the Christian Church, and Christian ministers, should sympathize with, and even unite themselves to, such an institution as this.

Suppose the church should conduct in this manner, and the Christian Church should receive its members in secret, and such oaths should be administered to them. Suppose Christianity would not allow its principles to be discussed, would not allow itself to come to the light, should use threats of assassination, and should actually resort to assassination to establish itself, and should thus create a feeling of terror throughout the whole world so that no man would dare to speak against it, to ventilate it, and show up its principles,—what would be said of Christianity, should it, like Freemasonry, take such a course as this?

The fact is, that Freemasonry is the most anomalous, absurd, and abominable institution that can exist in a Christian country; and is, on the face of it, from the fact that it will not allow its principles to be discussed and divulged, a most dangerous thing in human society. In nearly all the letters that I am receiving on this subject—and they are numerous—astonishment is expressed, and frequently gratitude and praise to God, that a man is found who dares publicly to discuss and expose the principles of the institution. Now, what is this? Have we an institution, the ramifications of which are entwining themselves with every fiber of our government and our institutions, our civil and religious liberties, of which the whole country is so much afraid that they dare not speak the truth concerning it?

What is this, thrust in upon human society and upon Christian communities, that can not be so much as discussed and its principles brought to light without threats of persecution and assassination? What honest man can witness such a state of things as this in our government without feeling his indignation enkindled?

Everything else may be discussed, may be brought to the light, may be held up to the public for their verdict; but Freemasonry must not be touched. Other institutions must stand or fall in the light of reason and of sound morality. If they are sustained at all they must be sustained by argument, by logic, by standing the test of thorough criticism. But Masonry must stand, not by argument, not by logic, not by sound reason, but must be sustained by persecution and murder. And so universally, as I have already said, is this known and assumed, as to strike men in every part of the land with such terror, that they dare not speak their minds about it.

And now, are we in this country to hold our peace? to hold out our hands and have the shackles put upon them? Is the press to be muzzled, and the whole country to be awed and kept under the feet of this institution, so that no man shall dare to speak his mind? God forbid! "Every plant," says Christ, "which my heavenly Father hath not planted shall be rooted up." The works of darkness shall be dragged to the light; and the power of this institution must be broken by a thorough expose of its oaths, its principles, its spirit and tendency. Afraid to speak out against such an abomination as this! Remember that he that would save his life by concealing the truth, and refusing to embrace and defend it, shall lose it.

Again, *Freemasonry is a most intolerant and intolerable despotism.*

Let any one examine their oaths, and see what implicit obedience they pledge to the great dignitaries, and Masters, and High Priests of their lodges, and they will see what an institution this is in a republican government. There is no appeal from the decision of the Master of a lodge. In respect to everything in the lodge, his word is law. In a recent number of the "*National and Freemason,*" which fell into my hands, the editor asserts that there is no appeal to the lodge from the decision of the Master of the lodge, and that he should allow none. In the ascending scale of their degrees, they swear to render implicit obedience to the grand lodges, and the higher orders above them, and this beforehand. They are not allowed to question the propriety of those decisions at all. They are not allowed to discuss, or to have any voice or vote in regard to those decrees. There is not in the world a more perfect and frightful despotism than Freemasonry is from beginning to end. Now, think of the great number of Freemasons in this country that are becoming accustomed to yield this implicit obedience to arbitrary power, a one man power, running through every lodge and chapter throughout the whole entangled system. And this institution is penetrating every community, selecting its men, and enforcing their obedience to arbitrary power throughout this whole republican country. And will not the country awake to this great wrong and this great danger? A friend of mine, a minister of the Gospel, writes me that he had been himself a Mason. He was urged to join the institution, as I was myself; but he renounced it many years ago, and supposed that it was dead. But some fifteen years since he found it reviving in the neighborhood where he was living, and he preached a sermon exposing it. That very week they burned him in effigy at his own gate; and that even now he could not preach against it and expose it without being set upon and persecuted he knows not to what extent.

And this, then, is the way for Masons to meet this question! If allowed to go on they will soon resort to mobs, as the slaveholders and their sympathizers did; and it will be found that Masonry can not be spoken against without mobs arising to disperse any assembly that may meet for the examination of the subject. If fifteen years ago a minister of the

Gospel could be burned in effigy before his own gate, for bringing this institution to the light, and if now threats of assassination come from the four winds of heaven if a man speaks or writes the truth concerning it, if let alone how long will it be before it will have its foot upon the neck of the whole nation, so that it will be sure to cost any man his life who dares to rebuke it?

But why do Freemasons take this course? Why do they decline to discuss, and resort to threats of violence? I answer first, for the same reason that slaveholders did the same.

Many years ago John Randolph, with a shake of his long finger, informed the Congress of the United States, that slavery should not be discussed there. At the South they would not allow tracts to be circulated, nor a word to be spoken against the institution. They resorted to every form of violence to prevent it. And who does not know the reason why? Their abominable institution would not bear the light, and they knew it right well. Freemasons know very well that they can not justify their institution before an enlightened public. I mean, those of them who are well-informed know this.

Multitudes of them are so ignorant as to feel quite sure that they are right, and that their institution is what it professes to be. The well-informed among them know better; and those who would naturally be expected to discuss the question, if it were discussed, know that they can not stand their ground. They can not justify their horrid oaths, with their barbarous penalties. They know that they can not establish their false claims to great antiquity.

The ignorant or dishonest among them will vapor, and set forth their ridiculous pretensions to antiquity; and will try to persuade us that God was a Freemason when He created the Universe, and that all the ancient worthies were Freemasons. But the well-informed among them know perfectly well that there is not the shadow of truth in all this pretension, and that their claim to great antiquity is a lie, and nothing but a lie, from beginning to end. They know also that the claims of the institution to benevolence are false, and can not be sustained, and that there is not a particle of *benevolence* in their institution.

Again, they know very well that the claim of Masonry to be a saving religion is a false claim; and that its claim to be substantially the Christian religion is without the least foundation. They know also that its professions are false in regard to the truth of history; and that its claim to be a depository of the sciences and arts is without foundation.

They know very well that Masonry has no just claims to be the light of the world in regard to any of its pretensions. They know that the secrecy which it enjoins can not be defended, and that it has no right to exist as a secret, oath-bound institution. They know that this oath-bound secrecy can not be justified before an enlightened public; that there is nothing in Freemasonry to justify their oaths or penalties, and that there is nothing in it that deserves the respect of the public.

They are well aware that they can not justify their pompous titles, their odious ceremonies, their false teachings, their shameful abuses of the Word of God; and they are ashamed to attempt to justify the puerilities on the one hand, or the blasphemies that abound on the other.

Any one who will examine Richardson's "Masonic Monitor," will find in it diagrams of the lodges and of many of the ceremonies; and if anybody wishes to see how ridiculous, absurd, and profane many of their ceremonies are, let him examine that work.

The reason of their declining all discussion, and resorting to threats of violence, is manifest enough. It is sagacious in them to keep in the dark, and to awe people, if they can, by threats; because they have no argument, no history, no anything that can justify them in the course they take.

Shame on an institution that resorts to such a defense as this? But it can not live where the press and speech are free; and this its defenders know right well. If freedom of speech is allowed on the subject, and the press is allowed to discuss and thoroughly to ventilate it, they know full well that the institution can not exist. The fact is, that Freemasonry must die, or liberty must die. These two things can not exist together. Freemasons have already sold *their* liberty, and put themselves under an iron despotism; and there is not one in a thousand of them that dares to speak against the institution, or really to speak his mind.

I have just received a letter from one of them, which reads as follows: "Dear Sir,—I merely write you as a man and professed Christian to say that you are doing God service in your attacks upon the institution of Masonry. I am a Mason, but have long since been convinced that it is a wicked, blasphemous institution, and that the Church of Christ suffers from this source more than from any other. You know that the oaths and scenes of the lodge are most shamefully wicked; and a Christian man's character, if he leaves them, is not safe in the community where he lives. You can make what use you please of this; but, perhaps, my name and place of residence had better not be made public, for I fear for my property and my person." This is the way that multitudes of Freemasons feel. They have sold their liberty, and they dare not speak out. Shall we all sell our liberties, and allow Masonry to stifle all discussion by a resort to violence and assassination? Threats are abundant; and they go as far as they dare do in *executing* their threats.

In some places, where Freemasons are numerous and less on their guard, I am informed that they do not hesitate to say that they intend to have a Masonic government, *peaceably if they can.* That this is the design of many of the leaders in this institution, there can be no rational doubt in the minds of those who are well informed. The press, to a great extent, is already either bribed or afraid to speak the truth on this subject; and, so far as I can learn, there are but few secular or religious papers open to its discussion. Now, what a state of things is this! A few years ago it was as much as a man's life was worth to write anything against slavery, or to speak against it, in the Southern States. And has it come to this, that the North are to be made slaves, and that an institution is to be sustained in our midst that will not allow itself to be ventilated? For one I do not feel willing at present to part with my liberty in this respect —although I am informed that a Mason, not far from here, intimated that I might be waylaid and murdered. It matters not. I will not compromise the liberty of free speech on a question of such importance to save my life. Why should I? I must confess that I have felt amazed and mortified when so many have expressed astonishment that I dared to speak plainly on this subject, and write my thoughts and views.

Among all the letters that I have received on this subject, I do not recollect one in which the writer does not admonish me not to publish his name. And this in republican America! A man's life, property and character not safe if he speaks the truth in regard to an institution which is aiming to overshadow the whole land, and to have everything its own way! as the writer of the letter from which I have just made an extract says, that a man's character is not safe if he speaks the truth concerning Freemasonry. Is not this abominable?

So well do I understand that Masons are

sworn to persecute, and to represent every one who abandons their institution as a vile vagabond, and to say all manner of evil against him, that I do not pretend to believe what they say of that class of men.

When the question of Freemasonry was first forced upon us in our church, and I was obliged to preach upon the subject and read from Bernard's "Light on Masonry," I found before I got home that Elder Bernard had been so misrepresented and slandered that people were saying, "He is not a man to be trusted." Who does not know that whoever has dared to renounce that institution, and publish its secrets to the world, has either been murdered, or slandered and followed with persecution in a most unrelenting manner?

## CHAPTER XIX

## RELATIONS OF MASONRY TO THE CHURCH OF CHRIST.

WE are now prepared to consider the question of the relation of Freemasonry to the Church of Christ. On this question I remark:

1st. God holds the church and every branch of it, responsible for its opinion and action in accordance with the best light, which, in his providence, is afforded them. This, indeed, is law universal, equally applicable to all moral agents, at all times and in all places. But at present I consider its application to the Church of God. If any particular branch of the church has better means of information, and therefore more light on moral questions, than another branch, its responsibility is greater, in proportion to its greater means of information. Such a branch of the church is bound to take a higher and more advanced position in Christian life and duty, to bear a fuller and higher testimony against every form of iniquity, than that required by less favored and less informed branches of the church. They are not to wait till other branches of the church have received their light, before they bear a testimony and pursue a course in accordance with their own degree of information.

2d. While Masonry was a secret, the church had no light, and no responsibility respecting it. Although individual members of the church, were Freemasons, as a body, she knew nothing of Masonry; therefore she could say nothing of it, except as its results appeared to be revealed in the lives of individuals; and, in judging from this source of evidence, the church could not decide, if the lives of the members were good or bad, whether it was Freemasonry that made them so; because, of its nature, designs, principles, oaths, doctrines, secret practices, she *knew nothing*. Hence God did not require the church to bear any testimony on the subject as long as Masonry was a secret. The world did not expect the church to take any action, or to bear any testimony on the subject, as long as Masonry was a thing unknown, except to the initiated. In those circumstances the unconverted world did not expect any testimony from the church, and they had no right to expect it. The well-known fact, that many professed Christians were Freemasons, was then no disgrace to the Church of God, because the character of Freemasonry was not known.

3d. But the state of the case is now greatly changed. Freemasonry is now revealed. It is no longer a secret to any who wish to be informed. Its nature, character, aims, oaths, principles, doctrines, usages, are in print, and the books in which they are revealed are scattered broadcast over the land. As long ago as 1826, Wm. Morgan published verbatim the first three degrees of Masonry. That these degrees were faithfully published as they were known, and taken in the lodges, no man can truthfully deny. Two, or more spurious editions of this work have been published, for the sake of deceiving the public. To obtain a *correct* edition of this work is at present difficult. Just previous to the publication of this work, Elder Stearns, a Baptist minister, and a high Mason, one who had taken many Masonic degrees, a man of good character who is still living, had published a volume entitled "An inquiry into the nature and tendency of Speculative Freemasonry." In 1860 the same author published a volume entitled " Letters on Freemasonry, addressed chiefly to the Fraternity," with an appendix. He has recently published another volume, entitled "A new chapter on Freemasonry." Soon after the publication of Morgan's book, already referred to, a body of seceding Masons, appointed a committee of sixteen, if I do not mistake the number, upon which committee were several ministers of Christ, to prepare and publish a correct version of forty-eight degrees of Freemasonry. Elder Bernard had taken a large number of degrees, I know not exactly how many. The degrees ordered to be published by this committee were carefully collected and arranged and published under the following title, "'Light on Masonry:' A collection of all the most important documents on the subject of Speculative Masonry, embracing the reports of the western committees in relation to the abduction of Wm. Morgan, proceedings of conventions, orations, essays, etc., etc., with all the degrees of the order conferred in a Master's lodge as written by Capt. Wm. Morgan, all the degrees conferred in the Royal Arch Chapter, and Grand Encampmenof Knights Templar, with the appendant orders as published by the convention of seceding Masons, held at Leroy, July 4th and 5th, 1828. Also, a revelation of all the degrees conferred in the Lodge of Perfection and fifteen degrees of a still higher order, with seven French degrees, making forty-eight degrees of Freemasonry, with notes and critical remarks by Elder David Bernard, of Warsaw, Genesee County, New York, once an intimate Secretary of the Lodge of Perfection. This book soon passed through seven editions. An eighth, but an abridged edition, has been recently published in Dayton, Ohio." Since the publication of Bernard's book, a volume has been published, entitled "Richardson's Monitor of Freemasonry;" being a practical guide to the ceremonies in all the degrees conferred in Masonic Lodges, Chapters, Encampments, etc., explaining the signs, tokens and grips, and giving all the words, passwords, sacred words, oaths, and hieroglyphics used by Masons. The ineffable and historical degrees are also given in full. By Jabez Richardson, A. M. In this book are published sixty-two Masonic degrees, with diagrams of lodges, and drawings representing their signs and ceremonies. Brother Avery Allyn has also published a large number of Masonic degrees. The question of the reliability of these works, I have discussed in a previous number. I am a little more particular in naming them in this place, for the information of those who have not seen the books. The substantial accord of all these authors, and their *reliability*, seems to be established beyond all reasonable question. Now, since these revelations are made, and both the church and the world are aware of what Masonry really is, God demands, and the world has a right to expect, that the church will take due action and bear a truthful testimony in respect to this institution. She can not now innocently hold her peace. The light has come. Fidelity to God, and to the souls of men, require that the church, which is the light of the world, should speak out, and should take such action as will plainly reveal her views of the compatibility or incompatibility of Freemasonry with the Christian religion. As God's witnesses, as the pillar and ground of the truth, the church is bound to give the trumpet no uncertain sound, upon this question, that all men may know, whether, in her judgment, an intelligent embracing and determinate adhering to Freemasonry are compatible with a truthful profession of religion.

4th. The Church of Christ knows Masonry through these books. This is the best and most reliable source of information that we can have, or can reasonably ask. We have seen in a former number, that Freemasons do not pretend that Freemasonry has been substantially altered since the publication of these books, that we have the most satisfactory evidence that it has not been, and can not be substantially changed. Let it therefore be distinctly understood, that the action and testimony of the church respects Freemasonry as it is revealed in these books, and not as *individuals* may affirm of it, *pro* or *con.* By these books we know it. By these books we judge it, and let it be understood that whatever action we take upon it, or whatever we say of it, we both act and speak of Masonry as it is here revealed, and of no other Masonry or thing, whatever. To this course, neither Masons nor any one else can justly take exceptions. From all the testimony in the case, we are shut up to this course. Let not Freemasons complain of this. These books certainly reveal Masonry as it was forty years ago. If it has been changed, the burden of proof is on them, and inasmuch as they make no pretense that Masonry has been reformed, and in view of the fact, that they still maintain that they embrace all the principles and usages of ancient Freemasonry, we are bound to speak our minds of Freemasonry as these books reveal it.

5th. Judging then, from these revelations, how can we fail to pronounce Fremasonry an anti-Christian institution? For example, 1st, We have seen that its morality is unchristian. 2d. Its oath-bound secrecy is unchristian. 3d. The administration and taking of its oaths are unchristian, and a violation of a positive command of Christ. 4th. Masonic oaths pledge its members to commit most unlawful and unchristian deeds. *a.* To conceal each others crimes. *b.* To deliver each other from difficulty whether right or wrong. *c.* To unduly favor Masonry in political actions and in business transactions. *d.* Its members are sworn to retaliate, and persecute unto death, the violators of Masonic obligation. *e.* Freemasonry knows no mercy, but swears its candidates to avenge violations of Masonic obligation even unto death. *f.* Its oaths are profane, the taking of the name of God in vain. *g.* The penalties of these oaths are barbarous and even savage. *h.* Its teachings are false and profane. *i.* Its design is partial and selfish. *j.* Its ceremonies are a mixture of puerility and profanity. *k.* Its religion is Deistic. *l.* It is a *false* religion, and professes to save men upon other conditions than those revealed in the Gospel of Christ. *m.* It is an enormous falsehood. *n.* It is a swindle, and obtains money from its membership under false pretenses. *o.* It refuses all examination, and veils itself under a mantle of oath-bound secrecy. *p.* It is a virtual conspiracy against both Church and State. No one, therefore, has ever undertaken, and for the plainest reasons none will undertake, to defend Freemasonry as it is revealed in these books. Their arguments are threats, calumny, persecution, assassination. Freemasons do not pretend that Freemasonry, as revealed in these books, is compatible with Christianity. I have not yet known the first Freemason who would affirm that an intelligent adherence to Freemasonry, as revealed in these books, is consistent with a profession of the Christian religion. But we know, if we can know anything from testimony, that these books do truly reveal Freemasonry, We have, then, the implied testimony of Freemasons themselves, that the Christian Church ought to have no fellowship with Freemasonry as thus revealed, and that those who adhere intelligently and determinately to such an institution have no right to be in the Christian Church. In our judgment we are forced to the same conclusion, we can not escape from it, we wish it were otherwise, we therefore sorrowfully, but solemnly, pronounce this judgment.

6th. Every local branch of the Church of Christ is bound to examine this subject, and pronounce upon this institution, according to the best light they can get. God does not allow individuals, or churches, to withhold action, and the expression of their opinion, until other churches are as enlightened as themselves. We are bound to act up to our own light, and to go as far in advance of others as we have better means of information than they. We have no right to say to God that we will act according to our own convictions, when others become so enlightened that our action will be popular and meet their approval.

Again: Those individuals and churches, who have had the best means of information, owe it to other branches of the church, and to the whole world, to take action and to pronounce upon the unchristian character of Freemasonry, as the most influential means within their reach of arousing the whole church and the world to an examination of the character and claims of Freemasonry. If churches who are known to have examined the subject withhold their testimony; if they continue to receive persistent and intelligent Freemasons; if they leave the public to infer that they see nothing in Freemasonry inconsistent with a creditable profession of the Christian religion, it will be justly inferred by other branches of the church, and by the world, that there is nothing in it so bad, so dangerous and unchristian as to call for their examination, action, or testimony. Before the publishing of Morgan's book, the Baptist denomination, especially, in that part of the country, had been greatly carried away by Freemasonry. A large proportion of its eldership and membership were Freemasons. A considerable number of ministers and members of other branches of the Christian Church had also fallen into the snare. The murder of Wm. Morgan, and the publication of Masonry consequent thereupon in the books I have named, broke upon the churches—fast asleep on this subject—like a clap of thunder from a clear sky. The facts were such, the revelations were so clear, that the Baptist denomination backed down, and took the lead in renouncing and denouncing the institution. Their elders and associated churches, almost universally, passed resolutions disfellowshiping adhering Masons. The denomination, to a considerable extent, took the same course. Throughout the Northern States, at that time, I believe it was almost universally conceded, that persistent Freemasons, who continued to adhere and co-operate with them, ought not to be admitted to Christian churches. Now it is worthy of all consideration and remem brance, that God set the seal of His approbation upon the action taken by those churches at that time, by pouring out His Spirit upon them.

Great revivals immediately followed over that whole region. The discussion of the subject, and the action of the churches took place in 1827-'8 and '9, and in 1830 the greatest revival spread over this region that had ever been known in this or any other country. They knew Masonry, as we know it, by an examination of those books in which it had been revealed. We have the same means of knowing Freemasonry, if we will use them, that those churches and ecclesiastical bodies had. We have the highest evidence that the nature of the case will admit, that God approved of their decision and action. In the brief outline that I have given in the preceding pages, I have endeavored to show truthfully, so far as my space would allow, what Freemasonry really is, and if it is what these books represent it to be, it seems to me clear as noonday, that it is an anti-Christian institution. And should the question be asked, "What shall be done with the great number of professed Christians who are Freemasons?" I answer, Let them have no more to do with it. Again, let Christian men labor with them, plead with them, and endeavor to make them see it to be their duty to abandon it. These oaths should be distinctly read to them, and they should be asked whether they acknowledge the obligation of these oaths, and whether they intend to do the things that they have sworn to do. Let it be distinctly pressed upon their consciences, that all Masons above the first two degrees have solemnly sworn to conceal each other's crimes, murder and treason alone excepted, and all above the sixth degree have sworn to conceal each other's crimes, without an exception All above the sixth degree have sworn to espouse each other's cause and to deliver them from any difficulty, whether they are right or wrong. If they have taken those degrees where they swear to persecute unto death those who violate their obligations, let them be asked whether they intend to do any such thing. Let them be distinctly asked whether they intend still to aid and abet the administration and taking of these oaths, if they still intend to countenance the false and hypocritical teachings of Masonry, if they mean to countenance the profanity of their ceremonies, and practice the partiality they have sworn to practiced. If so, surely they should not be allowed their places in the church.

## CHAPTER XX.

### CONCLUSION.

IN concluding these pages I appeal to Freemasons themselves. Gentlemen, I beg you to believe that I have no personal ill-will toward any member of your fraternity. Many of them are amongst my personal acquaintances, and some of them nearly related to me.

I have written of Masonry, I pray you to remember, as revealed by Wm. Morgan, also Avery Allyn, Elders Bernard and Stearns, and Mr. Richardson. That these authors truly reveal Masonry I am certain, so far as I have personal knowledge of it. That they truly reveal the higher degrees I have as good reasons for believing, as of any fact to be established by human testimony. You can not justly expect me to doubt the truthfulness of these revelations. You must be aware that God will hold me responsible, and demand that I should, in view of the testimony, yield my full assent to the credibility of these authors. You must know that God requires me to treat this subject in accordance with this revelation. Now, gentlemen, no one of your number has attempted to show that these books are not substantially reliable and true. No one of you has appeared to publicly justify Masonry as revealed by these authors. You must be aware that no man *can* justify it. No respectable author amongst you has attempted to show that Freemasonry has undergone any essential improvement, or modification, since these revelations were made; but on the contrary the most recently published Masonic authorities assert or assume that Masonry has not been changed, and that it is still what it ever has been, and that it is insusceptible of change, as I have *proved* it to be. Now, my dear sirs, what *ought* you to expect of me? To hold my peace and let the evil overrun the country until it is too late to speak? Believing, as I most assuredly do, that these works truly reveal Masonry, could I be an honest man, a faithful minister of Christ, and hold my peace in view of the alarming progress that this institution is making in these days. In your hearts you would condemn and despise me if, with my convictions, I suffered any earthly considerations to prevent my sounding the trumpet of alarm to both Church and State. Would you have me stultify my intelligence by refusing to believe these authors; or, believing them, would you have me cower before this enormously extended conspiracy? Or would you have me sear my conscience by shunning the cross, and keeping silence in the midst of the perils of both Church and State? And, gentlemen, can you escape from the conclusions at which I have arrived. Granting these works to be true, and *remember I am bound to assume their truthfulness*, can any of you face the public and assert that men who have intelligently taken and who adhere to the horrid oaths, with their horrid penalties, as revealed in these books, can safely be trusted with any office in Church or State? Can a man who has taken, and still adheres to the Master's oath to conceal any secret crime of a brother of that degree, murder and treason excepted, be a safe man with whom to entrust an office? Can he be trusted as a witness, a juror, or with any office connected with the administration of justice? Can a man who has taken and still adheres to the oath of the Royal Arch degree be trusted in office? He swears to espouse the cause of a companion of this degree when involved in any difficulty, so far as to extri

cate him from the same, whether he be right
or wrong. He swears to conceal his crimes,
*murder and treason not excepted.* He swears
to give a companion of this degree timely
notice of any approaching danger that may
be known to him. Now is a man bound fast
by such an oath to be entrusted with office?
Ought he to be accepted as a witness, a juror—
when a Freemason is a party, in any case—
a sheriff, constable, or marshal; ought he to be
trusted with the office of judge or justice of
the peace? Gentlemen, you know he ought
not, and you would despise me should I not be
faithful in warning the public against entrust-
ing such men with office. But further: Take
the large class of men who have sworn, under
the most awful penalties, to take *vengeance* on
all who violate Masonic obligations; to seek
their condign punishment; to kill them; to
persecute them, and to ruin them by representing them wherever they go as worthless
vagabonds. Now, gentlemen, I appeal to you,
is a man who is under a most solemn oath to
kill or seek the death of any man who shall
violate any part of the Masonic oaths a fit
person to be at large amongst men? Why,
who does not know that Freemasons are in the
habit of violating various points and parts of
their Masonic oaths, and are not Freemasons

bound by oaths to kill them, or seek their death? There are many seceding Masons throughout the land. Adhering Masons are under oath to seek to procure their death. Now if they adhere to their oaths and thereby affirm that they *design* to fulfill their vows, if an opportunity occurs, ought they not to be imprisoned or put under the heaviest bonds to keep the peace? No one can face the public and deny this, admitting as he must that their oaths are truly recorded in these books. No one can think this conclusion harsh unless he assumes contrary to all evidence, either that no such oaths have been taken, or if they have, and are still adhered to there is no danger that these vows will be fulfilled. Take these books and say wherein have I dealt harshly or uncharitably with Freemasonry as herein revealed? Ought a Freemason of this stamp to be fellowshiped by a Christian Church? Ought not such an one to be regarded as an unscrupulous and dangerous man? I appeal to your conscience in the sight of God, and I know that your moral sense must respond amen to the conclusions at which I have arrived. Be not offended with my telling you the truth in love. We must all soon meet at the solemn judgment. Let us not be angry, but honest

# EWorld Inc.
## Send for our complete full color catalog today!

| Title | Author | Price |
|---|---|---|
| A Book of The Beginnings Vol. I & II (set) | Massey | 49.95 |
| Afrikan Holistic Health | Afrika | 19.95 |
| African Discovery of America | Weiner | 15.95 |
| Anacalypsis (set) | Massey | 49.95 |
| Arab Invasion Of Egypt | | 16.95 |
| Ankh: African Origin of Electromagnetism | | 10.95 |
| AIDS The End of Civilization | Douglass | 9.95 |
| Baby Names: Real Names with Real Meanings for African Children | | 12.95 |
| Black Heroes of The Martial Arts | Van Clief | 16.95 |
| Apocrypha (hc) | | 14.95 |
| British Historians & The West Indies | Eric Williams | 14.95 |
| Christopher Columbus & The African Holocaust | John Henrik Clarke | 10.95 |
| Columbus Conspiracy | Bradley | 14.95 |
| Dawn Voyage: The Black African Discovery of America | Bradley | 14.95 |
| Documents of West Indian History | Eric Williams | 15.95 |
| Education of The Negro | Carter G. Woodson | 14.95 |
| Egyptian Book of The Dead | Budge | 16.95 |
| Egyptian Book of The Dead/Ancient Mysteries of Amenta | Massey | 9.95 |
| First Council of Nice: A World's Christian Convention A.D. 325 | | 10.95 |
| Forbidden Books of The New Testament | | 14.95 |
| Gerald Massey's Lectures | | 10.95 |
| Global Afrikan Presence | Edward Scobie | 15.95 |
| Gospel of Barnabas | | 14.95 |
| Greater Key of Solomon | | 10.00 |
| Hairlocking: Everything You Need To Know | Nekhena Evans | 9.95 |
| Harlem Voices from the Soul of Black America | John Henrik Clarke | 10.95 |
| Harlem USA | John Henrik Clarke | 10.95 |
| Heal Thyself for Health and Longevity | Queen Afua | 18.95 |
| Heal Thyself Cookbook: Holistic Cooking with Juices | Diane Ciccone | 13.95 |
| Historical Jesus & the Mythical Christ | Gerald Massey | 9.95 |
| History of The People of Trinidad & Tobago | Eric Williams | 15.95 |
| Lost Books of The Bible & The Forgotten Books of Eden | | 14.95 |
| Nutrition Made Simple; At A Glance | | 8.95 |
| Signs & Symbols of Primordial man | | 17.95 |
| Vitamins & Minerals A to Z | Jewel Pookrum | 13.95 |
| What They Never Told You In History Class Vol. One | Cush | 19.95 |
| Freemasonry Interpreted | | 12.95 |
| Freemasonry & The Vatican | | 11.95 |
| Freemasonry & Judaism | | 11.95 |
| Freemasonry: Character Claims | | 13.95 |
| Freemasonry Exposition: Exposition & Illustrations of Freemasonry | | 9.95 |
| Science of Melanin | | 14.95 |
| Secret Societies & Subversive Movements | | 13.95 |

**Prices subject to change without notice**

Mail To: EWorld Inc. – 1200 Jefferson Ave. – Buffalo – New York – 14208
TEL: (716) 882-1704  FAX: (716) 882-1708  EMAIL: eeworldinc@yahoo.com

NAME:_____
ADDRESS_____
CITY_____ST_____ZIP_____